George C. Blasiola II

Koi

Everything about Selection, Care,
Nutrition, Diseases, Breeding,
Pond Design and Maintenance,
and Popular Aquatic Plants

With 71 Color Photographs;
50 Illustrations by Michele Earle-Bridges

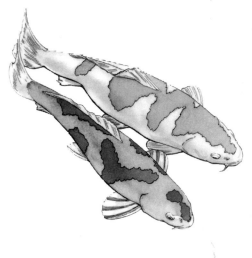

BARRON'S

Dedication

This book is dedicated to my dear friend Sue Busch, pet-industry leader and benefactor, whose vision, leadership, and commitment to pet-care education have helped make the American pet industry stronger.

All inquiries should be addressed to:
Barron's Educational Series, Inc.
250 Wireless Boulevard
Hauppauge, NY 11788

International Standard Book No. 0-8120-3568-2

Library of Congress Catalog Card No. 95-7036

Library of Congress Cataloging-in-Publication Data

Blasiola, George C.
    Koi : everything about selection, care, nutrition, diseases, breeding, pond design and maintenance, and popular aquatic plants / George C. Blasiola.
        p.   cm.
    Includes bibliographical references (p. 102) and index.
    ISBN 0-8120-3568-2
    1. Koi. I. Title.
    SF458.K64B58 1995

    639.3′752—dc20   95-7036
                                                                                      CIP

Printed in Hong Kong

5678 9955 98

About the Author

George C. Blasiola II, B.S., M.A., is a specialist in fish biology. He was formerly associated with the Steinhart Aquarium, California Academy of Sciences, San Francisco as an aquatic biologist. As chief koi consultant to the City of San Jose, Japanese Friendship Gardens from 1975 to 1985, he helped redesign the extensive pond systems and set up a comprehensive fish health husbandry program for the city's koi collection. He is currently the Vice President of AquaDine Nutritional Systems Inc. He has published more than 90 articles on fish health, pond management, parasitology, fish biology, and related topics in scientific journals and popular magazines. His research has focused on the identification and control of diseases of pond and marine fish, and on the role of nutrition in preventing the development of such disease.

Blasiola has been an annual lecturer at the University of Georgia's Fish Health Workshop since 1982. He has lectured at various professional meetings including the American Fisheries Society; the International Association of Aquatic Animal Medicine; the University of California, Davis; Hayward State University; Musee Oceanographique, Monaco; the Australian Rainbow Fish Association, Sidney; Texas A & M University (AquaMed); Oregon State University, and the D.C. Association of Veterinary Medicine.

He is contributing editor to *Freshwater and Marine Aquarium Magazine* and *Pet Age*, a review board member for the *Journal of Aquaculture and Aquatic Sciences*, and the author of Barron's *New Marine Aquarium Handbook*.

Acknowledgements

The author extends his appreciation to the following individuals who were helpful in preparation of this book: Tom Graham and Joyce Conrad of *Koi USA* magazine for their assistance in koi identification and generous contribution of photos; Bob Spindola for supplementary koi photo identification; Dr. Robert Rofen for use of the Aquatic Research Library facilities; Verle Parker, librarian for assisting with reference materials; Wyatt LeFever of Blue Ridge Fish Hatchery for his assistance in providing information and photos of the butterfly koi; Dr. John B.Gratzek for use of the carp pox photo; Scott Massey for his contribution of southern regional koi pond photos; Robert Weiss of AquaDine, for his support of this project; Don Reis and the Barron's staff for their professionalism; and Michele Earle-Bridges for the preparation of the superb illustrations.

Photo Credits

Blue Ridge Fish Hatchery: pages 12, 24; *Koi USA:* pages 16–23, 31, 40 (center left), 72; Scott Massey (Animal Kingdom): pages 33, 37, 40 (bottom left and right), 41, 48 (bottom), 68; University of Georgia: 92 (left).

All other photos were taken by the author.

Important Note

Before using any of the electrical equipment described in this book, be sure to read Avoiding Electrical Accidents on page 34.

Contents

Preface

Koi come in such a diversity of beautiful colors and patterns that this alone would be sufficient reason for cultivating an interest in these fish. In addition, they are hardy and relatively easy to maintain. Thus, the practice of keeping koi in beautiful garden ponds continues to increase in popularity year after year.

Koi, as the major animate element in a water garden, bring an enhanced appreciation of nature. Their gentle disposition and relative ease of care make them one of the world's favorite ornamental fish. A short walk in a garden to relax and enjoy nature is immeasurably enhanced by the sight and sound of koi rushing to their feeding area. The calm feeling that this produces will be eagerly anticipated at the end of a busy day.

Unlike many other types of fish, koi are extremely hardy and can survive for long periods in less than favorable conditions. However, it is important to provide responsibly for one's living charges, and this means understanding their requirements and giving them the best care possible.

This book offers the basic information needed for maintaining koi in an optimal aquatic environment. Mastering its contents will help you ensure the long-term survival of your fish.

George C. Blasiola II
Spring, 1995

A collection of healthy koi that delight visitors to the Japanese Tea Gardens in San Jose, California.

A History of Koi Varieties

Koi, or *nishikigoi* (Japanese for "colored koi"), are the most popular freshwater fish among pond owners. Their beauty, grace, and brilliant colors have made them one of the world's favorite ornamental fish. Because they combine ease of care, longevity, adaptation to most pond environments, and often striking color variations, they are eagerly sought after by owners throughout the world. Over the past several decades, new varieties (types) have become available for stocking ponds. So brilliant are their colors that some have referred to them as "living jewels."

Symbols of strength and masculinity in Japan, koi are known there as the "warrior's fish." The Japanese also regard them as symbols of good luck and prosperity. Each year in the month of May, beautiful *koinobori* (streamers) in the shape of koi are flown from poles in celebration of the Boy's Day Festival. The streamers symbolize the Japanese parent's hope that their sons will demonstrate courage and strength, like that of the *nishikigoi*.

Due to the large number of color variations and patterns, koi are sometimes thought to be different species, yet they are all *Cyprinus carpio*. There are some apparent exceptions, such as the novel butterfly koi, but these are hybrids created by mating closely related carp. The numerous varieties available today are the result of careful selective breeding conducted over many centuries.

The Ancient Period

Koi have a long and intriguing history that has been embellished with myth and story. There are conflicting opinions as to the precise point at which the first color varieties were observed and by whom. The exact date will probably never be known, and much of what passes as history is speculative.

Some authorities believe that koi originated in Persia and were spread by various peoples throughout the ancient world. Eventually they were introduced to China and Japan.

The ancestors of present-day koi varieties are known to have been drab in color. Known as the common carp, *Cyprinus carpio*, and called *magoi* by the Japanese, these unremarkable gray fish inhabited streams, foraging on plant materials and sifting the bot-

All koi are descendants of the drab-colored common carp that inhabited streams in Europe and Asia.

om for food. They were rugged and hardy, endowed with the ability to withstand various water conditions. As a result, they successfully colonized various habitats. Wild carp were and are an important food source in various parts of the world, especially in Asia and Europe.

One of the first references describing koi with colors is from a Chinese book written during the Western Chin Dynasty, 265–316 A.D. It describes carp with black, blue, red, and white coloration. Although the Chinese are thought by some historians to have played a role in the early development of color varieties, the exact sequence is only speculative. Some "ichthyhistorians" dispute whether the Chinese were ever involved in the early development of koi varieties, although they certainly were instrumental in the development of numerous fancy goldfish.

The details of early Chinese involvement may never be satisfactorily resolved, but we do know that it was the Japanese who eventually became the leaders in selective breeding of koi. Today, the Japanese are still preeminent in the field.

The Modern Period

Koi breeding began in the seventeenth century in the rice-growing region of Niigata Prefecture, Japan. Farmers there developed an interest in wild carp after noticing that from time to time the gray fish would have offspring that differed in color and body patterns. By carefully selecting for unusual forms and color patterns over many generations, they were able to establish a number of koi varieties.

By the nineteenth century, with an increased number of farmers interested in breeding koi, many new color varieties were being developed in the region. The popular *kohaku* line was established during this period. The once-wild fish, used only for food, was firmly on the road to becoming a fashion statement—and eventually, the "fish of the nobility."

At the turn of the twentieth century, koi were known only among the farmers of the Niigata region. This changed in 1914, when some of the most beautiful varieties were exhibited at an exposition in Tokyo. This marked the first time that koi were seen by people outside of the Niigata villages. Some of the best koi were presented to Crown Prince Hirohito. From this point on, interest in these fish exploded, eventually establishing their popularity throughout Japan and other parts of the world.

Later, as major pedigree lines were stabilized, additional new varieties were developed. A number of varieties were developed during the Japanese Taisho era (1912–26) and the early years of the Showa era (1926–89). (Japanese eras are named for the reigning emperor.) The *ki utsuri* variety was developed during Taisho, and the *ginrin* and *Showa sanke* during Showa. Although koi are now bred all over the world, the Niigata region is still the most active area for the development of new varieties.

Skilled koi breeders have a deep understanding of inheritance and genetics, and through many years of experience are continually producing koi with new color variations and patterns. Each year, additional varieties are developed and brought to market. Breeding fish of certain pedigree lines are especially prized and command large sums of money. It is not unusual for a top-quality koi to sell for as much as $15,000 to $20,000. Pedigree koi have been sold for even more in Japan, with values climbing into the hundreds of thousands of dollars.

Koi began to become popular in the West during the 1950s. During the 1980s a renewed interest in ornamental garden ponds, coupled with the

The Niigata Prefecture is the principal area for breeding koi in Japan.

development of better filtration techniques, induced more and more people to become interested in koi. The availability of liners made it easier to construct a pond, and increased breeding of koi made the fish more readily available.

Note: Although the Japanese term *nishikigoi* is technically correct, all varieties, whether single or multicolored, will be referred to in this book as koi.

Koi often appear in oriental paintings and carvings. This koi is one of several depicted in a large Chinese painting on silk.

Koi thrive in well-maintained outdoor ponds where they are often the focus of attention for children on school outings.

Morphological Features of Koi

Koi are bony fishes, classified as *Cyprinidae*, a closely related family that includes goldfish and minnows. Their scientific name is *Cyprinus carpio*. Ornamental koi are domesticated carp that have been selectively bred for their colors and patterns. They are freshwater, bottom-dwelling fish, inhabiting temperate climes but capable of living in a wide range of conditions.

The rounded body is fusiform in shape (thickest in the middle and tapered toward the ends), with a pair of barbels (threadlike appendages) hanging from the sides of the snout. Koi are excellent swimmers and can dart away quickly if threatened by a predator.

Wild carp, the ancestors of the koi, are found in lakes and streams throughout the world. They feed on plants, worms, insects, etc. Carp can reach a length of over 3 feet (.9 m) and weight in excess of 25 pounds (11.3 kg).

Koi are long-lived fish, with individuals known to have survived well over 40 years. However, reports of Japanese koi living to an age of over 200 years are probably more myth than fact.

General External Features

Koi have the structural features common to all bony fish, as well as several features characteristic of the species.

Medial fins are all single. The large dorsal (top) fin, which extends backward, is lowered during rapid swimming and helps maintain the fish upright in the water. The forked caudal (tail) fin is used to propel the fish forward. On the koi's ventral (bottom) surface a single anal fin helps to stabilize the fish during swimming.

Lateral fins are paired. The pelvic fins, located in front of the anal fin, enable the fish to move up and down in the water. And just behind the gill covers are the pectoral fins, which are used in braking and making turns.

The mouth is located at the end of the snout, slightly below the midline. This position allows koi to feed efficiently on bottom materials.

The barbels are richly endowed with sensory receptors that enable koi to detect food particles in sand or mud without the need for visual information. Just above the barbels, almost between the eyes, are a pair of nostrils which are used to detect odors.

Ears: Koi possess organs of hearing similar to other vertebrates, but there are no external "ears." The internal ear detects sound in association with the swim bladder. Sound causes the swim bladder to vibrate, and these vibrations are transmitted in turn to the *otoliths* of the inner ear. Auditory nerves are then stimulated and the signals sent to the brain. As with other vertebrates, the inner ear and otoliths are also important in maintaining equilibrium and balance.

Lateral lines: Close examination of the sides of the koi will reveal a series of small pores that run approximately midline from head to the tail. These are termed the *lateral lines*. Their purpose is to detect low-frequency vibrations in the water, such as might be generated by a large predator.

The eyes are located behind the nostrils. Koi lack true eyelids, the cov-

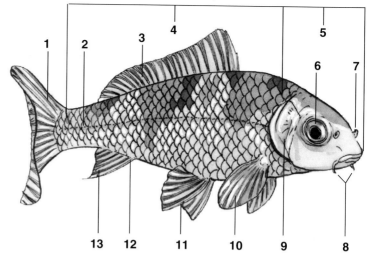

1. Caudal fin
2. Lateral line
3. Dorsal fin
4. Body
5. Head
6. Eye
7. Nostril
8. Barbels
9. Operculum
10. Pectoral fins
11. Pelvic fins
12. Anal pore
13. Anal fin

The external morphological features of a koi, Cyprinus carpio.

ering of the eye being simply a layer of transparent *epithelium* (skin). The lens is spherical and rigid, providing focus by moving forward or back within the eye.

Gills are respiratory structures situated behind the eyes in *branchial chambers*. Each set of gills is covered by a flap of skin and bone called an *operculum*, which moves water across the feathery gills. The gills themselves contain specialized tissues with rich capillary networks designed for gas exchange. Dissolved oxygen is taken in from the water and carbon dioxide and ammonia are released.

Scales: The body is typically covered with a large number of small scales, though there are breeds that have a lesser number of large scales, and others in which the scales are absent. When examined microscopically, scales appear to have a series of concentric rings that have been used to help determine the approximate age of the fish. However, interpretation of the rings is often difficult as they represent periods of growth, which may or may not be correlated directly with

years. Scale-ring analysis, therefore, cannot be used to derive an absolute age for any given specimen.

The scales, when present, overlap and project out of the dermal layer (skin) at an angle. They are covered with a layer of mucus, which reduces friction as the fish swims. It also offers some protection from bacterial and viral infections, both as a physical barrier and by the presence of antibodies within the mucus.

The colors of koi are a function of the type and distribution of pigments within the fish's skin. Within certain of the dermal cells are tiny sacs of pigment called *chromatophores*. These pigment sacs can contain several types of pigments, including *melanin* (black) and the *carotenoids* that give the beautiful and well-known red and orange colors. In addition to these pigments, koi also have cells called *iridocytes*, which contain guanine crystals. It is these crystals that give the silver or gold metallic appearance to the koi's skin.

When examined under high magnification, the chromatophore cells appear to have highly branched processes connected to nerve fibers. This feature allows a change in color. If a koi is stressed from poor water quality or illness, it may change its color and become lighter or darker simply by the movement of pigment granules within the cell. If the pigments move into the center of the cell, the animal becomes lighter. Conversely, if the pigments move out into the outer processes, the fish becomes darker.

General Internal Features

The internal organs of koi are similar to those of other bony fishes. They include components of the digestive, excretory, circulatory, and reproductive systems.

Digestive system: Koi and related cyprinids have long intestinal tracts and lack true stomachs. The length of the intestine correlates with their predominantly vegetarian diet.

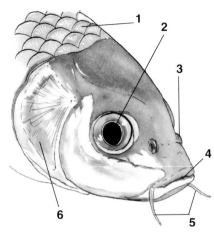

1. Scales
2. Eye
3. Nostril
4. Mouth
5. Barbels
6. Operculum

A closeup of the koi's head region. Note the characteristic barbels.

(Carnivorous animals, both terrestrial and aquatic, have comparatively shorter intestines.) Food is ground as it passes through the pharyngeal teeth in the back of the throat. Then it

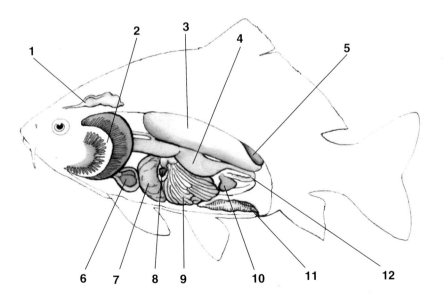

1. Brain
2. Gills
3. Swim bladder
4. Stomach
5. Kidney
6. Heart
7. Liver
8. Gall Bladder
9. Pyloric caeca
10. Spleen
11. Anal pore
12. Intestines

The internal anatomical features of the koi.

travels through the esophagus to the gut where it is digested by enzymes and other secretions, some of which are provided by a large liver.

Excretory system: The waste products of digestion are released through the anus, just anterior to the anal fin. The gills also function as excretory organs, releasing ammonia and carbon dioxide.

Like other freshwater fishes, koi have the problem of eliminating the excess water that is constantly entering the bloodstream through the gills and other body surfaces. This function is served by a kidney located close to the vertebrae. Along with excess water, liquid wastes filtered by the kidney are eliminated through the anus.

Circulatory system: The two-chambered heart, situated behind the gills, is enclosed in a pericardial sac. It pumps blood through arteries which extend throughout the fish's body. The arteries subdivide until they become the microscopic capillaries It is in through the capillaries that interchanges between the tissues and the blood occur. Then the capillaries reunite forming the veins, which carry blood back to the heart. Because it allows deoxygenated blood from the periphery to mix with reoxygenated blood from the gills, a two-chambered heart is less efficient than a four-chambered mammalian heart. As a result, the oxygen content of the fish's blood is more diluted, and its metabolism slower than that of mammals.

Swim bladder: The function of this organ is to control the fish's buoyancy and therefore its depth in the water. It is a large, air-filled organ located dorsal to the intestine near the backbone. It also serves as a sound receptor.

The swim bladder can be subject to various problems that can cause the fish to have difficulty in maintaining its normal buoyancy. This is often associated with systemic bacterial infections.

Butterfly koi have a beautiful silvery and gold metallic sheen due to special cells in their skin called iridocytes.

Varieties and Types of Koi

Basic Koi Classification

All koi, regardless of their color patterns, are scientifically classed as carp, *Cyprinus carpio*. However, a multitude of breeding programs have created a wide range of morphological varieties. As the largest number of breeders are Japanese, it is typically Japanese conventions that govern classification, and Japanese names and terminology that are usually employed.

The Japanese classify koi varieties according to various features, including color, patterns, and scale type and arrangement. There is an economic and esthetic hierarchy of form, color, and pattern that determines the desirability and value of a particular fish.

Though there are great subtleties involved in the esthetic judging of these animals, some of the more common varieties are not difficult to characterize. Certain features remain consistent within each variety, permitting easy assignment of a given koi to a recognized group.

Japanese terminology ranges from down-to-earth description to poetic analogy to political reference, but as the actual words used to discuss these animals are typically untranslated Japanese, the meaning of the names is frequently lost to the western fancier. While the intricacies of breeding are important to advanced hobbyists, the new fancier will need first to master the basics of physical care. Only after one becomes an expert in keeping koi alive and well can one give any serious thought to the possibilities of breeding, for which a knowledge of the many varieties would be essential.

With this consideration in mind, only a brief summary of the classification system and a limited amount of terminology will be covered in this work.

Koi Terminology Explained

All the major varieties have their specific names, and subsets within the variety will have their own names as well. For example, a certain major variety, the *kohaku*, has red and white markings, while another major variety, the *sanke*, has black and red patterns on a white background. There is a subvariety known as the *Taisho sanke*, "Taisho" indicating that it was developed during the reign of that emperor. Another subvariety is the *tansho kohaku*. This red-and-white fish with a large red mark on its head borrows its name from the red-crested crane.

Names can also refer to specific coloration patterns. An example of this is a *kohaku* with a cluster of red spots. This particular type is referred to as a *gotenzakura*, which translates as "palace cherry blossoms."

Coloration: As a general rule, koi will bear from one to three body colors. Various koi represented in the single-color koi group include:

- orange *ogon* (orange)
- *ki-goi* (yellow)
- *shiro* (white)
- *muji* (flat)
- *ogon* (metallic)

Koi in the double-color group are described by names which can be one or two words. In binomial appellations the second word refers to the background color of the fish. The term "background" is given to the color that occupies the greatest area of skin. A common koi variety in this group, widely available and familiar to many pond owners, is the previously mentioned red and white *kohaku*. Other varieties in this two-color category include *shiro utsuri* (white and black), *shiro bekko* (black and white), and *ki utsuri* (yellow and black). The word *utsuri* means reflection. Therefore the koi variety

ki-utsuri translates to "yellow koi with a reflection."

The third group consists of koi varieties with three body colors. These koi represent some of the most popular pond varieties. They include the *Showa sanke* (black background with white and red mottles) and *Taisho sanke* (white background with black and red mottles).

Patterning: The Japanese also employ terms to describe specific patterns of coloration. For example, there is a popular *kohaku* (red and white) with a pattern on its back that resembles lightning. It is called *inazuma hi* (red lightning). Another example is the previously mentioned *tancho kohaku*, with red markings on the top of its head.

Scalation: The scale pattern (or absence of scales) is an additional characteristic used in describing koi. In some varieties it is the dominant esthetic consideration. An example would be the *doitsu* (German-scaled), a hybrid of German and Japanese koi. This is a type with a reduced number of scales, first bred in Germany during the early 1900s. Some of these fish were eventually introduced into Japan, where they were crossed with Japanese koi. *Doitsu* have large, sparse scales. Occasionally the scales are entirely lacking, and the fish are then referred to as "leather koi."

Doitsu are subdivided into types and include *kani goi*, which are scaleless; *kagami goi*, which have large scales on the dorsal and ventral portions of the body; and *ara doitsu*, which have large scales with an irregular arrangement all over the body.

It is important to note that *doitsu* characteristics can be found in any color classification. For example, a *kohaku* pedigree of the *doitsu* type would be called a *doitsu kohaku*, the word *doitsu* used as a prefix to the varietal name.

1. Black marking
2. White background
3. Red marking
4. Border line

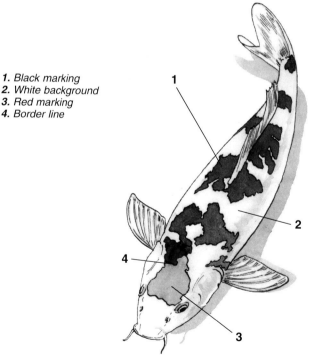

Body patterns are one of the characteristics used to classify koi. The tancho sanke *has a white background, black patterns, and a red patch on its head.*

Varieties and Types

While there are a limited number of major koi varieties, there are numerous subvarieties or *types*. To the Japanese, many of these types are considered to be of "low quality" if they lack desirable characteristics of the varietal group. It is important not to consider the groupings synonymous with "pedigrees," as this is not always the case with koi. It is the actual physical characteristics of a given koi that determine its classification, not its pedigree line. However, the classification system does include a "catch-all" group. This is the *kawari mono* classification, in which are placed all koi not fitting into any other variety group.

It should be mentioned that the popularity of types is subject to the vagaries of fashion and changes from time to time. As new varieties are developed, some older types may experience a decline in popularity, and the parameters of "quality" can change accordingly.

The Classification System

The Japanese classification system is a complicated one. It is basically comprised of thirteen major varieties, which are used consistently for judging koi during competitions.

The following varieties are recognized, although others will undoubtedly be added in the future as new strains are developed.

1. *Asagi* and *Shusui*
2. *Bekko*
3. *Hikarimoyo mono*
4. *Hikari utsuri mono*
5. *Kawari mono*
6. *Kinginrin*
7. *Kohaku*
8. *Koromo*
9. *Ogon*
10. *Showa sanke*
11. *Taisho sanke*
12. *Utsuri mono*
13. *Tancho*

Scalation is also an important characteristic in koi classification. From top to bottom: doitsu *(leather scale type)*; normal scale; doitsu *(mirror scale type)*.

1. *Asagi* and *Shusui*

These two varieties of koi are traditionally combined in one category during Japanese koi competitions.

Asagi ("light blue") are predominantly blue or gray on their backs, while the underside is generally red or orange. The scales tend to be light in color and can be patterned in either the normal or *doitsu* types. First developed approximately 150 years ago, they are quite beautiful and a welcome addition to any pond.

Good-quality *asagi* must have a uniform blue coloration. The scales should be bordered in white, creating the overall appearance of a piece of netting. Areas of brilliant red coloration must be present on the base of the pectoral fins, the sides of the head, and the base of the dorsal and tail fins, but there should be no red on the dorsal portion of the fish. The

Asagi *koi were developed approximately 150 years ago.*

Shusui *are often quite striking fish with large* doitsu *scales and beautiful colors.*

Bekko *koi have patterns that resemble a tortoise shell. Note the characteristic black patches* (sumi) *on this* aka bekko.

dorsal head region is generally white or blue.

There are various types of *asagi*, of which the most important are:

Asagi sanke, which have an *asagi* pattern with red on the abdomen and head region and a white underside.

Konjo asagi, which possess a coloration ranging from dark gray to black. This type is rather out of favor among Japanese fanciers these days.

Mizu asagi, which are highly prized, light blue fish.

Taki asagi, which are blue on the back and red on the abdominal area, with an intersecting band of white.

Shusui ("autumn water") resemble *asagi koi,* but they occur only as *doitsu*. Large scales are found on the dorsal portion of the fish, beginning on the head and ending at the base of the tail. This type was developed from the *asagi* by Mr. Yoshigoro Akiyama, who mated a *doitsu* with an *asagi sanke*. A strikingly beautiful fish, the *shusui* has a bluish color on the back and is reddish underneath. It is eagerly sought after by koi owners.

To be considered of good quality, a *shusui* must have the proper alignment of large, dark-blue scales along the back. The scales should be offset by a lighter background, preferably white, while the head should be light blue. Red should be present on the snout, below and behind the eyes, at the bases of the fins, and on the abdomen. The Japanese consider *shusui* to be of inferior quality when gray, black, or other colors are present on the scales.

Some representative types include:

Hi shusui, which have a red color (*hi*) on the back. The large *doitsu* scales on the back are blue and extend from the head to the tail.

Ki shusui, which have the characteristic *shusui* body, but with yellow and dark blue on the back.

Hana shusui, which have red markings on both sides of the body and abdomen, extending to the tail.

Pearl shusui, having *doitsu* scales with a glittering pearly appearance.

2. Bekko

This variety was developed during the *Bunka* (1804–17) and *Bunsei* (1818–29) eras. It has patterns that resemble those of a tortoise shell. The primary color can be red, orange, yellow, or white, highlighted by black patterns on the upper body. Generally, a high-quality *bekko* should have black stripes on the pectoral fins and no black at all on the head region. Some types, however, depart from this ideal. Black patches, called *sumi*, should appear only on the back of the fish.

Variations within this category include:

Aka bekko, which have *sumi* on a basic red background.

Ki bekko, which have *sumi* on a yellow background.

Shiro bekko, which are primarily white with black sumi accents and no red markings. Black stripes can be present on the pectoral fins.

Doitsu bekko, which can have either scaleless "leather" bodies or mirror scales.

3. Hikarimoyo Mono

The Japanese word *moyo* translates as "pattern," while *hikari* means "metallic." Fish in this group will have two colors—one metallic, the other flat. The metallic color should be bright, meaning white fish should have a deep platinum color, black fish a jet black, and red fish the appearance of copper. The head region should be free of any spots, which are considered to be defects. For example, a platinum fish should not have black marks (*sumi*) on the head.

A beautiful shiro bekko *koi.*

This leather type koi is classified as a doitsu shiro bekko.

Hikarimoyo *are koi with two colors, one of which is metallic.*

Kin ki utsuri *koi are classified within the* hikari utsuri *group: koi that are bicolored with distinctive metallic scales.*

The goshiki *is a popular and highly prized fish among koi fanciers.*

Ginrin bekko *with a striking tortoise shell pattern.*

Several representative types within the grouping are:

Hariwake, which have gold and silver patterns on the body and fins. The head region is usually of one color and free of marks.

Kinsui, which have a metallic red coloration.

Yamabuki, which have a yellow and platinum coloration.

Yamatonishiki, a favorite of koi fanciers, which has a beautiful metallic appearance.

4. *Hikari Utsuri Mono*

The *hikari utsuri* group is comprised of bicolored fish with distinctive metallic scales. Other colors can be present, including black and red.

Quality in this group is based on rich metallic color, which should be clean and shiny, and clean patterns. Red fish should have a color that is bright and coppery, blacks should be deep and inky, and whites should have a platinum sheen. The head region of red and white fish should be free of any specks or markings.

Types within this category include:

Kin ki utsuri, which have a beautiful metallic yellow color.

Kin Showa, which have a metallic gold color, developed during the Showa era (1926–89).

Gin Showa, which have a silver or platinum color.

5. *Kawari Mono*

This is the "catch-all" term, as all koi that do not fit into other categories are placed within this group. Some of the types include:

Karasu goi, which have an overall black color ranging from light gray to deep black.

Ki goi, with a yellow body and variable coloration on the fins. They can possess normal or *doitsu* scalation, and, if the latter, can be either leather or mirror-scale type.

Kumonryu, a predominantly black type with an irregular white line on the back and sides. The pectoral fins can be either solid white or black and white. The name translates as "dragon with nine markings."

Goshiki, one of the most prized koi, distinguished by a combination of five body colors. This type is predominantly black with accents of red, white, brown, and blue. Goshiki are produced by crossing an *asagi* with an *aka sanke*.

6. Kinginrin

This group is also metallic, but the metallic sheen tends to be brighter with numerous silver body markings. The distribution and appearance of the silver on the scales is variable. The scales are also referred to by different names, depending on their characteristics. For example, scales that have a high luster and strongly reflect the silver color are called *beta gin*.

Variations are abundant in this group. Several common ones are:

Ginrin, whose silver-colored scales appear on the white portion of the fish's body.

Kinginrin bekko, a black fish with silver markings on the body scales.

Kinginrin kohaku, on which the red and white body has a scattering of silver on the scales, giving an interesting glittering appearance.

Kinginrin sanke, with silver scales on the red, black, and white body.

7. Kohaku

Among the most readily available koi, the *kohaku* has red color accents on a white background. The variety dates to around 1800. *Kohaku* are without a doubt the most popular koi among the Japanese.

Good-quality *kohaku* should have brilliant red markings on a pure white body color and a red pattern on the head. Fish with a yellowish tinge to

A stunning ginrin kohaku *with the characteristic metallic sheen on its scales.*

Kohaku *have red markings on a white background. This prize-winning* kohaku koi *is a superb example.*

This inazuma kohaku *is named for the lightning-like pattern on its back.*

19

Aigoromo *are produced by crossing an* asagi *with a* kohaku.

A yamabuki ogon.

A kin matsuba ogon.

the body are considered of lesser quality. The presence of black specks or marks, referred to as *sumi* or red marks on the snout and lips also lessen the quality of the fish. Their scalation can be either normal or *doitsu*.

There are numerous types occurring within this category, including:

Aka muji, a predominantly red fish.

Shiro muji, a predominantly white fish. Better-quality *shiro muji* are free of black spots or other dark pigmented markings.

Inazuma has a lightning-like pattern present on the dorsal surface of the fish, usually extending down the entire back. Higher-quality fish have an unbroken pattern with a good red color present.

Kuchibeni, which has red color present on the head region and on the lips. This type is not favored in Japan.

Nidan, which has two large red spots on the body.

Omoyo, which has a large, red wavy pattern on the back.

8. *Koromo*

This variety is less common than some of the others. It is characterized by red and white coloration, with an overlay of blue or silver over the background. *Koromo* translates as "robed," a description of the overall appearance of the color patterns. This variety is produced by breeding an *asagi* with other varieties, such as the *kohaku* or *Showa sanke*.

Some types within this group are:

Aigoromo, a hybrid produced by crossing an *asagi* with a *kohaku*. The fish has a distinctive blue edging on the red background.

Budo sanke, an uncommon type with a white background on which are found black and blue markings that give the appearance of bunches of grapes.

Koromo sanke, which have blue markings on the red areas of the fish's body. It is produced by breeding a *Taisho sanke* with an *aigoromo*.

9. Ogon

A well-known and popular variety, the *ogon* has a uniform metallic-gold body color varying in hue from light to dark. Good-quality *ogon* should not have a blackish cast on the body. Among the types within this group are:

Doitsu ogon, which can be either mirror scale or leather type.

Hi ogon, which have a red body color. The body area is generally uniform, with streaks of off-white to yellow.

Kin matsuba, a golden type with dark color present in the center of the scales, giving a reticulated appearance to the body. *Matsuba* translates as "pine-needles."

Ogon, which has a body coloration ranging from yellow to yellow-orange. Other *ogon* koi have a silvery color often referred to as platinum.

10. Showa Sanke

The Showa sanke, also referred to simply as *Showa*, is primarily black with red and white markings. It was developed by breeding a *kohaku* with a *ki utsuri*.

This variety can easily be confused with the *Taisho sanke*, described below. To differentiate them, bear in mind that the *Taisho sanke's* black coloration is present on the dorsal area, the pectoral fins are colorless, and black coloration is absent from the head region. The *Showa sanke's* black coloration, on the other hand, extends to the abdomen, while the pectoral fins and head are black.

Good quality *Showa sanke* must have deep red and black and bright white coloration. Black and red color will be present on the head, and there will be a black spot on the base of the pectoral fins. The Japanese refer to this black spot as *montoguro*.

A *platinum* ogon *of the leather* doitsu *type.*

The Showa sanke *group, also referred to as* Showa, *are koi with red and white markings on a black background.*

A doitsu showa.

21

The Taisho sanke *or tricolor has black and red accent coloration on a white body background.*

A beautiful Taisho sanke *with strong color patterns.*

Kuchibeni Taisho sanke *have red on the snout and lips.*

Types within this group include:

Boke Showa, which are lighter in color, and which may have a bluish appearance. The black coloration is usually not well-defined.

Doitsu Showa, with mirror-type scales, or none at all.

Hi Showa, in which red predominates on the dorsal portion and there is only a minor amount of white. The red color normally extends from the head region to the tail.

Kindai Showa, which resemble the *Taisho sanke* but have larger areas of white on the body. Black *sumi* markings are not found on the pectoral fins.

11. *Taisho Sanke*

The *Taisho sanke* is another popular koi variety. It is also referred to as a *sanshoku,* which translates as "tricolor." This variety was developed during the Taisho era (1912–26). It is characterized by a white background with black and red accent coloration.

Quality is determined by various factors, including the balance of the color patterns. The body should be bright white. A red pattern should be present on the head of quality specimens, preferably without *sumi* marks.

Several representative types within the *Taisho sanke* category include:

Aka sanke, which is mostly red.

Doitsu sanke, which have a small number of large mirror scales or no scales at all.

Kuchibeni, which have red on the snout and lips.

12. *Utsuri Mono*

This variety is distinguished by a black background and white, red, or yellow markings. The black pectoral fins tend to be triangular in shape. It is older than the *sankes,* having been developed during the Meiji era (1867–1912).

The body coloration should be a uniform black, with black present on

Shiro utsuri *display white markings on a black background.*

The tancho Showa *has the typical markings of a* Showa sanke *but with the* tancho *marking on the head.*

Hi utsuri *have red markings on a black background.*

A tancho sanke *with a strong tancho mark on the head.*

This is an excellent example of a tancho kohaku.

A tancho utsuri *displays a black background with a white pattern and a red* tancho *mark.*

With their shimmering metallic bodies and long flowing fins, these butterfly koi are extremely beautiful.

the pectoral fins and head, as well. Representative types include:

Shiro utsuri, with white body patterns.

Hi utsuri, with red body patterns.

Ki utsuri, with orange or yellow markings.

Doitsu utsuri, with scalation as described above.

13. *Tancho*

The body is a uniform white color, and there is a distinctive red pattern on the top of the head. Quality is judged by the uniformity and purity of the white background and the shape and extent of the head marking. Some varieties within the group include:

Tancho kohaku, in which the only red area is on the head.

Tancho Showa, which have the typical *Showa sanke* pattern (see above) with the distinctive *tancho* head mark.

Tancho sanke, with white body coloration, black patterns, and the *red tancho* head patch.

Nontraditional Varieties

The varieties and types discussed thus far are considered to be traditional. However, other types of koi have been developed, although these are banned from competition in Japan. The most striking of these is the butterfly koi.

Butterfly koi are not normally included in discussions of the koi varieties. They are a beautiful fish, characterized by long, flowing fins and a metallic body. Since their introduction their popularity has increased steadily.

The butterfly-koi breeding program originated in the United States in the early 1980s. At that time, Wyatt Lefever, owner of the Blue Ridge Fish Hatchery in North Carolina, was contacted regarding some unusual long-finned koi included with a shipment of fish. As it turned out, the fish were not koi at all, in the traditional sense, but hybrid Asian carp. They were light gray in color and not particularly attractive.

From a starting stock of a dozen fish, only four survived to reach the spawning stage. The remaining fish were crossbred with koi that had metallic coloration. Although most of the progeny were normal in body appearance, several were metallic, with long fins. The name "butterfly koi" was coined one day while the breeder was viewing the fish in his pond. The shimmering metallic scales and long flowing fins reflected light to give an illusion of butterflies.

Butterfly koi are readily available to the enthusiast. Despite their delicate appearance, they are quite hardy and are able to withstand colder temperatures better than many traditional koi.

Planning and Installing a Pond

Designing a Koi Pond

Koi have been successfully maintained in various types of containers and under varying conditions. A properly designed pond will provide a healthy aquatic environment. Consideration must be given to the pond type, material used for construction, and selection of equipment and type of filtration, among other factors. Standard guidelines should be followed when setting up a koi pond. Hasty design can result in high maintenance as well as costly modifications to the system.

Pond Types

A koi pond can be constructed from various materials, including plastic liners, preformed fiberglass, reinforced plastic, and concrete.

Plastic Liners

Plastic liners have become increasingly popular in recent years. A pond employing polyvinyl chloride (PVC) can often be installed over a weekend. Unlike the rigid design of preformed fiberglass, liners can be adapted to any shape. They are available in various sizes, colors, and thicknesses. A liner of 32 mil thickness can be expected to last up to 10 years.

Although plastic liners have the disadvantage of tearing on occasion, they can be repaired using special PVC glue and a patch of the liner material. Also, careful handling and limited use of maintenance equipment that could puncture the liner will minimize the problem.

Tip: It is important to use only liners approved for use with fish, as some types are unsafe. Industrial liners, including many of those sold at hardware stores and home improvement centers, are treated with algicides and other chemicals that are harmful to fish and water plants.

A properly designed koi pond will reduce maintenance and avoid the need for costly modifications.

HOW-TO:
Installing a Pond Liner

Installation is relatively simple, provided all the materials and tools are available prior to installation. Such ponds can easily be installed over a weekend; the pond plantings and edging can be completed later.

Pond Shape and Location

The first step is to decide on the location and desired shape of the pond. Several sketches can be made to help you decide on a pond shape. A rope or a garden hose can then be placed on the ground to help you visualize the selected shape. Once you are satisfied, mark the pond perimeter with stakes or secure the rope in place as a guide when you excavate for the pond.

Ponds can be circular, oval, or kidney-shaped. It is best to stay with a simple standard shape. Complicated designs will make installation of the liner much more difficult, possibly requiring you to weld several liners together. However, the welding process is not that difficult, provided you consult your pet store or garden center about the correct adhesive.

Determining the Pond Depth

Determine the required pond depth and the depth of any shelf areas you wish to have around the perimeter for plant containers. Then estimate the required size of liner, allowing an extra amount of material— at least 12 to 14 inches (30.5–35.5 cm) for an overhang. Your garden center or pet store can advise you on the

A rope or a garden hose is useful for determining the desired size and shape of a pond. Use a carpenters level frequently during pond excavation.

correct-size liner to purchase; simply provide them with the correct measurements.

Excavating for the Pond

Excavate the soil from the designated area, removing any stones, rocks, or debris that could cause punctures to the liner. If you are going to have a marginal shelf for marsh plants, start by using a shallow excavation for the shelf. Make the shelf approximately 9 to 10 inches (22.9–25.4 cm) wide and 8 to 10 inches (20.3–25.4 cm) below the water's surface.

Closely inspect the pond bottom and sides for jagged stones. If large roots from a nearby tree are found during the excavation, the area may not be the best site for the pond. Always use a carpenter's level to make sure that the pond

shelves are horizontal. It is recommended that you dig several inches deeper than the desired depth since a layer of sand will be placed on the bottom.

Pond Bottom Preparation

The bottom of the pond as well as the marginal shelf areas will require a layer of sand to protect the pond liner from being damaged. After filling any holes, simply add a layer of sand to the pond bottom and the shelf areas to a depth of approximately 1 to 2 inches (2.5–5 cm) to cushion the liner. Smooth and firm down the sand layer. Check again for any stones or materials and make a final check of the pond with a level.

Installing the Liner

Prior to installation, the pond liner should be warmed in

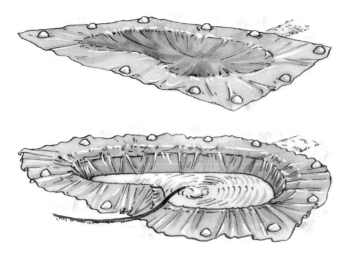

After excavation is completed, carefully drape the liner and secure it with rocks. Slowly fill the pond with water to prevent collapse of the liner.

edges, but leave at least 6 to 8 inches (15.2–20.3 cm) of excess, which can be covered with stone. Save any trimmings from the pond liner, as these can be used later for patching if there is a puncture or accidental tear. An edging of flagstone or rock can now be added to finish the pond perimeter.

If a large amount of materials have fallen into the pond during installation, drain the pond water and then refill. This is particularly important if you have used cement to join rocks or stones for the pond edging. The pond is now ready for conditioning the water, adding pond plants, and filtration start-up.

order to make it easier to place in the pond. This is done by unfolding or unrolling the liner and allowing it to lie in the sunlight for 20 to 30 minutes (depending on the outside temperature).

Install the pond liner, draping it loosely but fitting it to the contours of the pond. It is best to have the help of at least one or two other people to install the liner properly. Secure the liner around the pond perimeter with heavy stones. If required, you can fold and pleat the liner to fit into tight corners. Check the perimeter of the pond to ensure that it is level. Add soil underneath the liner and level again if necessary. Fill the pond with water, adding water slowly, a few inches at a time.

Completing the Installation

When the pond is full, trim any excess liner from the

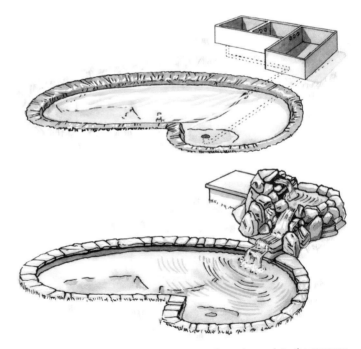

Secure the pond edge with flagstone or rock, and complete the preparations for the filter system. The finished pond is now ready for the introduction of koi.

Pre-formed fiberglass ponds are available in several shapes and sizes.

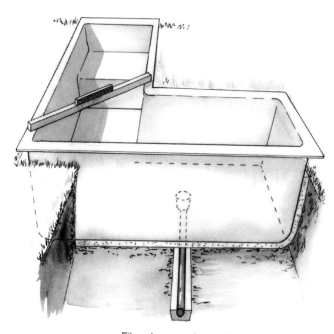

Fiberglass pond manufacturers will pre-drill the shell for filtration piping and drains. It is important to make sure that the pond is perfectly level during installation.

Rigid Fiberglass and Plastic Ponds

Fiberglass ponds, especially the preformed type, are very popular, due to their low cost and ease of installation. They are excellent for the neophyte.

Preformed fiberglass reinforced ponds are available in various sizes and shapes, including free-form and geometrics. They are weather-resistant and, depending on the material from which they are constructed, will generally withstand ice formation during the winter. Many suppliers will also pre-drill them for filtration piping and drains. Fiberglass ponds are an excellent way to get started with your first koi pond.

Preformed plastic ponds are generally too small to be considered for a koi pond. They are susceptible to deterioration when exposed to sunlight and tend to crack within a relatively short period of time.

Tip: Preformed plastic ponds are not recommended for use outdoors. They can, however, be used as emergency containers, or as temporary holding facilities and quarantine tanks.

Concrete Ponds

Concrete ponds can be custom-built to fit into any garden landscape. They are more costly to engineer and construct, but when properly designed they will outlast many other materials.

Concrete-pond styles can be formal or informal. Formal koi ponds have symmetrical shapes such as ovals, squares, or circles. By contrast, informal ponds can be of any shape—angled, curved, or both. Free-forms tend to be more popular these days, as such shapes can blend more easily into the landscape. Such "natural" ponds frequently incorporate raceways, waterfalls, and other features set into lush garden settings.

Whereas ponds constructed of most materials need only be rinsed before use, new concrete ponds require conditioning to neutralize the excessive amounts of lime that can leach into the water.

The standard procedure employs 70 percent technical grade phosphoric acid. This is added to the filled pond at a rate of ⅙ teaspoon (1 cc) per gallon (3.78 L).

Some type of agitation must be provided to ensure that the acid is evenly distributed throughout the pond. After two hours a pH test should be performed. Record the initial pH value. The pond water should be tested again after 24 hours, at which time the pH should be within the range of 2 to 4. It is important to maintain careful records during this time. If a filter has also been constructed from concrete, you can recirculate the water during the treatment period.

Perform a third pH test after another 24 hours. The pH will probably have increased to 5 or 6. If this occurs, add acid to bring the pH back down to 4. Continue adding and checking pH as often as necessary until the pH stabilizes at no more than 4. The pond conditioning period usually takes three to five days.

Once the pond surface and filter have been neutralized, the water should be drained and the pond rinsed thoroughly and refilled. Test the water after 24 hours. If the pH continues to decrease, phosphoric acid is still present in the pond. Drain off some water and add additional tap water. Retest. Once the water pH stabilizes you are ready to stock your pond.

Tip: Use caution when handling phosphoric acid and other chemicals. Gloves and eye protectors must always be worn. Be sure to avoid inhaling acid fumes, as lung damage can result.

Pond Size

Koi ponds must be designed to accommodate the size and number of fish you have selected, taking into

Concrete ponds are more costly to build but can be customized to just about any garden landscape. This pond was designed to withstand the cold winters in Cold Spring, New York.

consideration the fact that they will grow. As a general recommendation, ponds should not be any smaller than 300 gallons (1135 L). While it is possible to keep a number of koi in smaller volumes of water, maintenance of water quality is more difficult in smaller ponds. The smaller the volume, the more quickly the pond will foul. Small ponds will also undergo more extreme fluctuations in temperature. Crowding of koi must be avoided to minimize the stress and uncleanliness that predispose koi to disease.

Water Depth

A uniform pond depth must be avoided, as this poses problems in maintenance, water temperature fluctuation, and difficulty in protecting the fish from predators. Generally, the depth of the shallow zone should not exceed 20 inches (50.8 cm), sloping into water with a depth of about 36 inches (91.4 cm). Depths of 16 to 20 inches (40.6–50.8 cm) are sufficient in

The edging of any pond can be made more attractive by using flagstones or other native rock materials.

warm regions such as Florida, California, and Hawaii. In colder areas that are subject to freezing, water depths of 48 inches (1.2 m) or more may be required.

Shallow areas should slope at a steep angle into deeper pond zones. A deep central area of the pond allows for the gradual movement of debris toward that region, where it is more easily removed. A sump with a grate connected to a drain can be installed in nonliner-type ponds; this will remove debris to a sewer.

The range of depths will serve a number of purposes. Shallow areas around the edges of the pond can be used for observation and for feeding the koi. The shallow zones can also be used for planting various types of aquatic plants that are intolerant of deeper water.

Tip: Deeper zones in the pond serve as refuge areas where the koi can retreat from predators, as well as providing cooler zones during the summer months. In colder regions, deep areas provide a place where koi can hibernate during the winter months, safe from the layer of ice.

Pond Location

Ideally, koi ponds should be located in areas providing partial shade at some time during the day. Ponds situated in full sunlight often develop algae blooms, although sunlight is only one factor encouraging such developments. While it is impossible to eliminate the growth of nuisance algae, the proper location of the pond can help minimize this problem.

On the other hand, the pond should be located in an area free of over-hanging tree branches and bushes. While some vegetation can be planted nearby to provide some shade, the vegetation should not extend over the

A waterfall is a desirable pond feature, which provides water circulation and aeration.

Attractive pond landscapes require careful planning.

pond. In addition, make sure that the pond is not situated close to trees that could cause problems in the future. Developing tree roots will eventually crack nearby walkways and can cause damage to the pond structure. The decomposition of fallen leaves in ponds results in the development of acid conditions. The accumulation of organics in the bottom sediment promotes the development of anaerobic bacteria, which release toxic chemicals such as methane and hydrogen sulfide. Overhanging evergreens, such as spruce and pine, must be avoided. The falling needles leach toxic substances into the water.

In selecting a pond location you should also consider the accessibility of electrical connections. Electricity will be required for various pieces of equipment, including recirculating pumps for the filtration system and lighting.

Landscaping

It is important to prevent the entry of runoff water into the pond. Heavy water runoff carries organic materials, soil, fertilizers, insecticides, and other materials. The perimeters of below-grade ponds should be raised to prevent drainage from adjacent lawns during watering of plants and rainstorms. This can be accomplished by the installation of edging around the pond, using rock, wood, or other materials. It is essential to incorporate drains around the pond perimeter and nearby walkways to channel water away from the pond.

The most serious problem with water runoff is the potential accumulation of fertilizers and pesticides in the pond water. Fertilizers contain ammonium and phosphate compounds, and encourage algae development. Ammonium compounds also pose a

T*he perimeters of koi ponds should always be raised to prevent runoff from adjacent lawns. Popular materials include large rocks and wood.*

The use of water lilies and overhanging stone helps provide partial shade for the pond throughout the day.

Ponds should be located away from large trees since developing roots can eventually erode and crack walkways and pond structure.

direct threat to the health of the animals due to their toxicity.

Filtration Requirements

Filtration is necessary to minimize maintenance and to preserve a healthy pond environment. Although some ponds utilize a continuous influx of new water with constant draining of the old, this is prohibitively expensive and environmentally unsound unless you have access to an unpolluted stream.

The use of recirculated water through water purification devices (filters) is the most common method of conditioning. The selection of a proper filtration system is an extremely important decision for the koi pond owner. This is an area where you should not attempt to economize, as the ultimate success of the pond rests on the quality of the filter equipment. (A detailed discussion of filtration begins on page 47.)

Waterfalls must be carefully constructed and reinforced to prevent leaks, especially in colder climates.

Avoiding Electrical Accidents

It is important to use caution when handling electrical equipment and wiring, which are particularly hazardous when used in connection with water. Always observe the following safeguards carefully:

• Before using any of the electrical equipment described in this book, check to be sure that it carries the UL symbol.

• Keep all lamps away from water or spray.

• Before using any equipment in water, check the label to make sure it is suitable for underwater use.

• Disconnect the main electrical plug before you begin any work in a pond or touch any equipment.

• Be sure that the electric current you use passes through a central fuse box or circuit-breaker system. Such a system should be installed only by a licensed electrician.

• The installation of ground fault circuit interrupter (GFCI) on outside devices, especially those near the pond, is an important means of preventing accidental electrocution, both of yourself and of your koi.

Aeration

It is recommended that supplemental aeration be provided in ponds to maintain dissolved oxygen levels at acceptable concentrations. Large surface areas of ponds allow excellent gas exchange, but accessory agitation is always desirable. Chronically low dissolved oxygen concentrations reduce fish growth and increase the incidence of disease, which can lead to extensive koi mortalities.

Aeration accomplishes two important objectives:

• It maximizes the concentration of dissolved oxygen required by the fish and by the filter bacteria.

34

• It permits rapid dispersion of carbon dioxide and other gases from the water.

Tip: It is important to employ aeration devices when using well water. Water from this source is often low in oxygen, sometimes containing less than 1 part per million. Well water should be aerated to add oxygen and drive off any excess carbon dioxide. Aeration of new water can be accomplished through fountains, waterfalls, or other methods. It is important that the water be kept in motion. Stagnant conditions result in serious water-quality deterioration.

Care must be given to avoiding excessive agitation, however, since under certain conditions this can induce supersaturation of nitrogen, which can cause gas-bubble disease (see page 93).

In planning for accessory aeration, consideration should be given to the number of fish you place in the pond, as well as the type of filtration to be utilized.

Pond Skimmers

Ponds should incorporate some method of skimming the water to remove film, floating algae, and other materials that often collect on the pond surface. A pond skimmer will make maintenance easier by consolidating leaves and other floating debris in a collecting basket that can easily be cleaned. Skimmers are connected to the pump that pulls water into the filtration system.

Skimmers are generally incorporated into the design of concrete pools, and it is possible to incorporate them into other types of pools as well.

Water Evaporation

Because water is continually lost from ponds by evaporation, more will need to be added regularly to maintain the pond at a proper level. Although you can add water manually as needed, it is better to install an auto-

Common predators of koi include kingfishers, herons, weasels, and raccoons.

matic float valve. When the water level drops, the valve will automatically top off the pond. The basic requirements are access to a water supply and the various pipe fittings required to assemble the system. The valve should be located near an area of high water agitation, such as a waterfall, which will aerate new water as it is added and disperse any carbon dioxide.

Protecting Koi from Predators

A pond is a habitat that will inevitably attract wildlife. Although the presence of frogs and other small animals causes only minor problems, other animals can pose a serious danger. Koi spend much time near the water surface and are ready targets for predators, including birds such as herons and kingfishers, and mammals such as raccoons, foxes, cats, and badgers. Small juvenile koi and fry can easily be eaten by frogs and snakes.

Raccoons are particularly troublesome. As many homeowners can attest, these animals are intelligent and bold. They have the ability to

35

open trash cans or food-storage containers. In the evening raccoons will attempt to catch your koi and can damage plants such as lilies. They will spend time around the perimeter, reaching in to grab the fish. If a plant is large enough for them to leap to, they will do so. Make sure that potted plants are located away from the pond perimeter. No matter what you do to discourage raccoons, some will keep coming back. Therefore, the only way to prevent problems from them or other animals is to plan your koi pond properly.

Tip: Make sure the sides of the pond go down at a steep angle. Do not allow a gradual slope from the marginal shelves. If the shelves are used for pots of water plants, place the pots close together.

Depending on its location, your pond may also attract birds. Small birds such as sparrows are inconsequential. However, large predators such as herons and kingfishers can empty a pond of fish in no time at all. Kingfishers are particularly adept, setting a routine to feed on the smaller and medium-sized specimens in your koi collection. Once they have located the pond, they will return on a regular basis.

As a general rule, ponds should incorporate some means of preventing predators from getting near or into the pond. Providing deep-water areas and covering portions of the pond with a monofilament mesh stretched tightly over the pond, about 1 foot (30 cm) above the surface, should prevent most animals from getting to the fish. Electrical fences can also be installed around the perimeter of the pond and activated in the evenings. This is a very efficient means of discouraging some animals from coming near your pond. Others, however, may be able to jump over or otherwise circumvent the protective device.

Tip: Never run electrical fences on house current. A transformer must be used. Also, make sure you check local ordinances regarding the installation of such devices in your yard.

Some type of supplementary aeration should be provided in all ponds to facilitate gas exchange. This pond uses a simple fountain to agitate the pond water.

Aquatic Plants and Algae Control

Plants serve various functions in the pond. They add a natural aesthetic touch, provide shade, aid in water purification, and reduce the potential for growth of troublesome algae by competing with them for nutrients. Aquatic plants also provide hiding places for koi, especially juveniles, and provide areas for spawning. Koi like to attach their eggs to plants during the spring breeding season.

Not all plants will be suitable for the pond, as koi have a ravenous appetite for many common types. They especially like to root around the soil in containers and eat new shoots. A strategy must be followed to maintain koi and plants together in a pond.

Of the various types of aquatic plants suitable for use in koi ponds, water lilies, pond lilies, and lotuses are particularly recommended. Koi will generally leave lilies alone when they are properly planted and protected. Selection of plants will also depend on the geographical area in which you live. You should consult with a local nursery that supplies aquatic plants for information on selection and care.

Containers

Plants should not be planted in soil placed directly in the pond, but should rather be placed in tubs filled with a recommended soil mixture. Various types of containers are commercially available for use in the pond environment. They are made from several types of materials, including plastic, clay, and wood.

Using containers in the pond offers several advantages. They can be moved easily whenever you wish, such as during pond cleaning, or to take advantage of the best area and water depths for the plants. In addition, they are easy to remove for pruning, soil replenishment, or for indoor storage of delicate tropical plants during the winter.

Fertilizers must be kept to a minimum to prevent excessive addition of nitrogen and phosphates to the water. Bog plants, however, require refertilization every month.

Tip: Some of the best fertilizers for use in feeding aquatic plants are made in the form of sticks or coated beads that can be placed into the soil around the plant. They slowly release nutrients directly to the plant.

Basic Plant Categories

Water plants are traditionally divided into three categories: floating plants, shallow-water bog or marsh plants, and submerged plants.

A variety of these are readily available from garden centers and through mail-order catalogues.

Floating Plants

There are are two categories of floating plants: free-floaters, which have roots hanging freely in the water, and attached floaters, whose leaves float on the surface but whose roots are attached to the bottom. Floating plants are easy to care for and are efficient natural water filters,

Because of their easy care and attractive flowers, water lilies have become popular plants for koi ponds.

removing large quantities of nitrogen, phosphate and other substances from the water. They compete with algae for nutrients, thereby minimizing the chance of algal overgrowths.

Marsh and Bog Plants

Plants that grow in shallow water, with most of the plant above the surface, are included in this category. Many produce vegetation that is quite lush and varied. Bog plants grown in pots and scattered along marginal areas are beautiful additions to the pond. Popular plants include the arrowhead plant (*Sagittaria latifolia*), umbrella plant (*Cyperus alternifolius*), pickerel weed (*Pontederia cordata*), water iris (*Iris* spp.), sweet flag (*Acorus calamus*), and horsetail (*Equisetum hyemale*).

Submerged Plants

Submerged plants are rooted on the bottom, with their leaves totally below the surface. These plants are often sold for use in freshwater aquariums. Common examples include *Cabomba*, *Elodea*, and *Ludwigia*. Although they are excellent for removing nutrients and carbon dioxide from ponds, they are quickly uprooted and eaten by koi.

Popular Plants for Koi Ponds

Free-Floating Plants

Water fern (*Azolla caroliniana*): This floating plant is a fast grower, forming clumps of plants with crinkled-textured green leaves that turn reddish during the fall, and short, threadlike roots. The water fern prefers direct sunlight, but will tolerate some shade. The plant is sensitive to cold, and will die if the temperature drops below 50°F (10°C).

Water hyacinth (*Eichornia crassipes*): A tropical floating plant popular with pond owners, it is perennial in warm regions. Best treated as an annual in most of North America, it may also be taken indoors for over-wintering in colder climates. The plant has dark-green leaves with bulbous bases and bears compact stalks of blue or purple flowers. The short, trailing roots form a compact mass beneath the plant. One of its advantages as a floating pond plant is that it is an excellent natural filter, removing large quantities of nitrogen from water. Water hyacinths do best in full sun.

Water lettuce (*Pistia stratiotes*): This attractive floating plant forms rosette-shaped, compact leaf clusters, with a trailing, somewhat compact mass of roots. The plant is equally adaptable to sunny or shady areas of the pond. The plant occurs widely in the tropics, and under favorable conditions reproduces vigorously.

Attached Floating Plants

Water lilies (*Nymphaea* spp.): Undoubtedly the most popular of all aquatic plants, these provide a beautiful covering of leaves and a profusion of flowers. (Sometimes the related yellow pond lily—*Nuphar lutea*—is also called a water lily.) Both tropical and hardy varieties are commonly available for koi ponds. Tropical varieties must either be treated as annuals or taken indoors for overwintering in most of North America; hardy varieties can be left to overwinter outdoors. The lilies can either be planted in pots set on the pond bottom or placed in floating baskets. New plants should be anchored in pots, as the leaves and stems contain air pockets that permit them to float. Plants that have not taken root have a tendency to come loose when disturbed by fish. It is also recommended that new plants initially be placed in shallow areas of the pond, at least until a good growth has been established. The plants can then be progressively moved into deeper water as the leaves develop over time.

Containers are available in numerous shapes and sizes for planting aquatic vegetation.

Water lilies require at least six hours of sunlight per day.

Lotus (*Nelumbo spp.***):** One of the oldest cultivated water plants, lotuses bear some resemblance to water lilies, but they are in fact unrelated. The plants produce large leaves, often over 18 inches (45.7 cm) in diameter, and large flowers. During the growing period, the lotus first produces floating leaves which are followed by aerial leaves. The blooms are large, and often very fragrant.

Generally, lotuses are only suitable for large koi ponds due to their rapid growth rate and their large leaves that can cover the surface of small ponds. However, miniature varieties more suitable for smaller ponds have been developed. Like tropical water lilies, most lotuses need to be moved indoors during the winter season in colder climates. They can do well in cold as long as the water is deep enough to protect the growing portion from freezing. In regions of extreme cold, the pots can be taken in for storage after the leaves have died.

Tip: Store the pots in a cool area until spring, keeping the soil slightly moist.

Water poppy (*Hydrocleys nymphoides***):** A popular water plant, water poppies produce abundant oval green leaves and yellow flowers. They are capable of growing quickly and covering the water surface.

Water hawthorn (*Aponogeton distachyus***):** This plant, also known as Cape pondweed, produces leaves approximately 4 inches (10 cm) long. It prefers direct sunlight, but will tolerate some shade. Fragrant spikes of white flowers are produced during the winter or spring. By including these in the pond with water lilies, you will have some blooming plants in the pond during most seasons. Water hawthorn is perennial only in tropical to subtropical areas; it must be taken indoors for overwintering in temperate zones.

Shallow-Water Bog or Marsh Plants

Umbrella plant (*Cyperus alternifolius***):** Attractive tropical plants that thrive well in shallow pond environments, these plants are characterized by long, umbrella-like leaves at the end of long stems. In cold-weather climates, the plants must be brought inside for the winter.

Arrowhead plant (*Sagittaria latifolia***):** This is one of many species available for use in shallow zones of the pond. It has dark-green, arrow-shaped leaves, and bears spikes of white flowers.

Pickerel weed (*Pontederia cordata***):** This plant produces long-stalked, heart-shaped leaves that extend above the water. The flowers are blue and are borne on short spikes. It prefers full sun, and is an excellent marginal plant.

Water iris (*Iris spp***):** There are several species of water iris that are excellent for ponds. Irises have swordlike leaves ranging in color from light to dark green, and bear white, yellow, or blue flowers, depending on the species. They are best planted in wooden tubs or pots, submerged to cover the crown of the plant by several inches.

The Japanese water iris (*Iris kaempferi*) is a favorite among pond owners. It has foliage up to 4 feet (1.22 m) in length. Blossoms in various colors, including violet, purple, white, and blue, are produced in late May through June. They will thrive in either full sun or partial shade.

The purple water iris (*Iris laevigata*) produces deep-blue flowers with white markings. It also thrives in sun or partial shade, and blooms from spring to fall.

Horsetail (*Equisetum hyemale***)** is popular for use as a marginal plant. It produces slender, hollow, dark-green stems with circular dark rings. It is a fast-growing plant that does well in partial shade.

The water hyacinth, Eichornia crassipes, *is a popular floating pond plant.*

The lotus (Nelumbo *spp.) produces large, fragrant blooms.*

Tropical water lilies (unlike the hardy varieties) must be taken indoors for overwintering in colder regions.

The water poppy, Hydrocleys nymphoides, *grows quickly and produces attractive yellow flowers.*

Some species of water lilies are night bloomers, opening their blossoms only during the early evenings.

Water iris are easy-to-grow shallow water plants for the koi pond.

With proper care, lilies, lotuses, and other attached floating plants will flourish in your pond. Arrowhead plant, water iris, and other marsh species will do well around its edge.

This large koi pond uses water lilies and a variety of marginal plants.

A koi pond in Athens, Georgia with plantings of water lilies, water poppies, and arrowhead.

HOW-TO:
Planting Water Lilies and Lotuses

Water lilies should be planted in pots to protect them from being eaten by koi during their initial growing period. After selecting the container, add soil to fill about two-thirds or slightly less. Do not use commercially available potting soils, as these often contain large amounts of peat moss and other ingredients that will float to the pond surface. Ask for a mix that has been formulated for water lilies.

Place the lily root in the center of the container. Add fertilizer sticks or tablets around the roots, making sure that these do not come into contact with the root. Cover the root with soil, packing down to hold it in place. The growing portion of the lily (crown) should remain above the soil surface. Add enough small, pea-sized gravel, about ⅓ to ½ inch (8.5–12.7 mm), to fill the pot to the brim. This discourages the koi from digging around in the pot while the plant is establishing itself.

First obtain the necessary equipment—including soil, gravel, and fertilizer sticks or pellets.

The next step is to saturate the soil with water, being careful not to disturb the top layer of gravel. Then carefully lower the pot into the water and allow it to rest on the pond bottom. The lily's crown should not be deeper than 6 to 12 inches (15.2–30.5 cm). If necessary, you can place concrete blocks under the pot to maintain the plant at the acceptable water depth. Do not be concerned if some of the leaves are a few inches below the surface. They will reach the surface after a few days. Tropical varieties must

Carefully plant the lily in the soil making sure you do not cover the crown. Then add a layer of pea-sized gravel.

be moved indoors to overwinter in temperate areas.

Depending on the health of the plant and prevailing water conditions, it will take approximately three to four weeks for the plants to become acclimated and begin actively growing.

Lilies prefer water with as little disturbance as possible. They do well in areas with some movement but should not be placed in zones of continual water turbulence, such as near filters or aerators.

Place the container in the pond, raising it up to the proper water depth with bricks or concrete blocks.

Lotuses are planted in a manner similar to water lilies. Using a water-lily mix, add soil until the container is about half full, or slightly less. Place the lotus tuber in the center of the container. Add several fertilizer sticks or tablets, but make sure the fertilizer does not come into contact with the tuber. Cover with soil, packing it down to keep the tuber in place. The crown should be above the soil surface. Add enough small, pea-sized gravel, ⅓ to ½ inch (8.5–12.7mm) in diameter, to fill to the top of the pot.

Saturate the soil with water and lower the pot carefully into the water, allowing it to rest on the pond bottom. The ideal water depth will be 6 to 12 inches (15–30 cm). You can place concrete blocks underneath the pot to maintain the plant at an acceptable depth.

Lotuses, like lilies, prefer water with as little disturbance as possible. In addition, they will require fertilization (a few coated beads will be sufficient) at least once monthly.

A carefully designed marginal shelf permits beautiful landscaping of the pond border. In the deeper areas, various species of water plants including water lilies (Nymphaea *spp.*), lotus (Nelumbo *spp.*), and water poppies (Hydrocleys nymphoides) can be placed. The bog section is separated from the main pond by rocks, which allow some water to flow into the area creating a marshy environment. Plants such as the arrowhead (Sagittaria latifolia), water iris (Iris *spp.*), and cattails (Typha *spp.*), should do well in a properly maintained bog.

Pond plants have different water depth requirements. To assure their proper growth, follow the instructions given for the preferred depths. The level of the containers can be adjusted using either concrete blocks or bricks. Water lilies must not be planted too deeply. Bog plants should only be submerged for several inches. Always remember to add a sufficient amount of small pebbles on the top of newly planted vegetation to discourage koi from rooting around in the container and releasing sediments into the pond.

43

Acquiring New Water Plants

It is important to inspect and disinfect water plants before introduction to the pond to prevent possible transmission of certain fish diseases. Parasites, including microscopic larval forms, may be present on the plants, as well as snails, which can become pests. Many invertebrates also serve as carriers of intermediate stages of parasites.

Aluminum sulfate is a common disinfectant. A working solution is made by dissolving 1 teaspoon per quart (5 cc/l) of water and immersing new plants in the solution for not more than 10 minutes. Remove and rinse well. The plants can then be safely added to the pond without the fear of introducing parasites.

Tip: Caution should be exercised with aluminum sulfate, as this treatment may damage delicate plants. Always test several specimens before acquiring and treating a large number of plants with this or other chemicals.

Factors responsible for algal blooms include high nutrient concentrations, inadequate filtration, stagnant water, lack of shade, elevated water temperatures, and high pH.

Snail Control

Snails are likely to be introduced to the koi pond if plants are not carefully inspected or treated as recommended above. Many snails lay eggs on the plant surfaces, and these will appear as a gelatinous mass. For several reasons, snails are not desirable in koi ponds. Once established, they are quite prolific and can undergo a population explosion. As their numbers increase, they are adding to the biological load of your pond, consuming oxygen and adding waste products to the water. In addition, they destroy aquatic vegetation, preferring to eat the young, tender shoots of many plants. Finally, they can act as vectors for various diseases. Many species of snails act as intermediate hosts for parasitic worms such as digenetic trematodes.

If snails should inadvertently be introduced to your pond, they can be killed with various commercial products.

Warning: Many of these products contain copper as the active ingredient. Any copper-containing compound may harm both fish and plants!

Algae Control

Algae growth is one of the most common and annoying situations affecting pond owners. In the natural environment it is normal for algae to increase in early spring. As the season progresses, natural ponds clear on their own. Of course, such ponds are constantly being fed with a fresh supply of water that dilutes the nutrients that encourage algal growth. In any koi pond it is normal to have some algae growing on the bottom and sides of the pond. There are some advantages to this. Algae prevent the build-up of nutrients such as nitrate which normally accumulate in the pond water. They supply accessory oxygen during the day as a byproduct of photosynthesis, and also serve as an additional food source for your pond fish.

Algae become troublesome when pond conditions favor a population explosion. Rapid multiplication of algae depletes essential trace elements required by vascular aquatic plants such as water lilies. Overgrowth of such undesirable species as blue-green algae can overwhelm more desirable water plants. In the summer, when water temperatures are high, algae can rapidly deplete oxygen at night.

Algae Types

There are two types of algae, differentiated by their growth habits.

Phytoplanktonic or *pelagic* algae are single-celled microscopic plants that live suspended in the water. They prefer to concentrate in the upper portions of the water, where the temperature is higher and they are exposed to more sunlight. Their presence imparts a noticeable green color to water. This type is largely responsible for algal blooms in ponds. Various species can cause blooms, including *Palmella*, *Oscillatoria*, and *Anaebaena*.

Benthic algae, on the other hand, are generally attached to the pond bottom, though some forms can detach and float to the surface, where they form mats. Common types include the waternet, *Hydrodictyon reticulatum*, and the horsehair algae, *Pithophora oedogonia*.

Prevention is always preferred to using chemicals to control algal blooms. Understanding the causes of algal blooms can help to minimize or prevent serious pond problems. Major factors that initiate algal blooms are:

- High concentration of nutrients.
- Full exposure of pond to sunlight.
- Inadequate filtration.
- Lack of water movement.
- High pH.
- High temperatures.

Nutrients are, of course, required for algal growth and reproduction. Nitrogen and phosphorus are especially important. Accelerated algal growth rates correlate with high concentrations of inorganic nitrogen such as ammonia and nitrate. Many aquatic plants have a preference for ammonia and ammonium, but once these forms are exhausted, algae will utilize nitrogen in the form of nitrates. In koi ponds with excess amounts of decaying materials, which decompose into ammonia, algae rapidly absorb inorganic nitrogen. This results in a rapid population explosion—an algal bloom.

Aquatic plants are also highly efficient in the uptake of phosphorus. Overfeeding, allowing sediments to build up in ponds, and runoff from adjacent lawns all contribute to the buildup of both nitrogen and phosphorus.

Light exposure: Ponds exposed to full sunlight for the entire day will often experience algal blooms. On the other hand, ponds that are located in areas of partial shade seldom have this problem.

There are several strategies available for reducing sunlight to avoid excessive algal growth. First, use adequate and appropriate water plants such as water lilies, water iris, and water poppies to provide some shade. Providing a covered deck to shade a portion of the pond, or planting trees and shrubs in surrounding areas (but not overhanging the water) also will help reduce sunlight.

Filtration and water movement: As mentioned previously, koi ponds should always be equipped with a filtration system. A properly functioning system purifies the water, removing toxic nitrogen compounds such as ammonia. Still pond water favors the growth of algae. Good water movement and aeration can be provided by using a fountain or waterfall. Having good water movement in the pond keeps water temperatures more uniform and discourages the growth of algae.

High pH and temperature: Several water parameters are known to be instrumental in favoring algal growth, the most important being pH and temperature. It is known from extensive research that various species of algae, notably blue-green types, favor water with a higher pH because various nutrients, such as phosphorus, are more readily utilized when the water is alkaline. As for temperature, the warmer the water the faster the algae will grow. Ponds with elevated temperatures are more likely to develop algal blooms.

Preventing Algal Blooms

In general, algal blooms can be prevented if specific recommendations are followed in the initial design of the koi pond (see page 30). If algal blooms do occur, several solutions are available.

The first thing to do is to reduce the nutrient and algae load immediately by changing the water. Slowly add water to the pond, while allowing excess water to drain off until the pond water clears. The addition of water must be slow enough to prevent temperature or pH shock to the fish. However, this will provide only a temporary solution. You will need to find and correct the factors that produced the situation in the first place (e.g., reducing the amount of sunlight on the pond, increasing the number of vascular plants, decreasing the number of fish).

Tip: If you are using tap water, it has probably been treated with chlorine or chloramine. You will need to use water conditioners to destroy these toxic chemicals.

Algicides

Numerous commercial products are available for treatment of ponds. Approved products sold in the U.S.A. are registered with the Environmental Protection Agency (EPA). It is important to follow the instructions on the product carefully. Improper applica-

tion of algicides can damage or kill tropical plants such as water lilies.

Under most circumstances, use of algicides is not recommended. The decomposing algae increase the demand for oxygen in the pond, and deoxygenation can result in fish mortality.

Simizine: A common algicide used for the control of algae is 2-chloro-4, 6-bis-(ethylamino)-s-triazine, commonly marketed as Simizine. It is sold under various tradenames.

Tip: Simizine should only be used during early spring, before the onset of an algae bloom. Care should be exercised to ensure that treated water is not permitted to be used for irrigation, as it will kill plants other than algae.

Copper compounds can also be used for algae control. They are available in either liquids or powders. Copper-based products should also be carefully used according to the manufacturer's instructions, as copper can be toxic to plants and animals. The copper tolerance of fish is variable, depending on the species. Koi are known to tolerate concentrations up to 0.3 mg/l (ppm). However, as with all chemicals, toxicity varies with water conditions, especially pH.

Potassium permanganate, one of the oldest pond algicides, is rarely used to control algal blooms. However, the chemical is still sold under various tradenames. With the advent of better and safer algicides, potassium permanganate products are no longer recommended.

Important note: Algicides should be used only when all other means of algae control have failed. The reoccurrence of excessive algae indicates some malfunction in the koi pond design or deterioration of water quality. The goal should be to correct these problems prior to heavy reliance on the regular addition of chemicals to pond water.

Filtration and Pond-Water Quality

Optimal water quality is essential to the success of your koi pond. Although it is possible to maintain just a few koi in a pond without a filter, this procedure is potentially dangerous in the long term. Such ponds will function for a time, but eventually will begin to show accelerated deterioration in water quality. Filtration must therefore be considered mandatory to ensure a healthy aquatic environment for your koi.

Types of Filtration Systems and Processes

Depending on their design, pond filtration systems can be divided into three general categories: closed, semi-closed, and open.

Closed pond systems are defined as those in which the water is recirculated and purified by filter devices. Closed systems utilize biological filtration, supplemented with chemical and mechanical methods. Such systems rely primarily on the filter devices to maintain water quality, with additional water added as needed to replace loss to evaporation.

Semi-closed systems utilize a means of minimal filtration, but are supplemented by the constant, regulated addition of fresh water. Semi-closed pond systems are uncommon, primarily due to the cost of constantly adding water. In addition, the new water must be treated before addition to the pond to detoxify harmful chemicals such as chlorine.

Open systems are those in which the water is purified by the constant addition of new water and draining of the old—much like a natural pond fed by a stream. This would be a perfect method for maintaining optimal water quality were it not for the fact that it is prohibitively expensive. An additional problem is the need to detoxify the chlorine or chloroamine in large amounts of tap water. And finally, local regulations in areas subject to recurring droughts might make it impossible to rely on this type of system for purifying pond water.

Filtration Processes

The actual processes by which water is cleaned are classified into three types: *biological*, *chemical*, and *mechanical*. All three play an important role in contributing to good water quality. Ideally, closed systems should utilize all of these methods to maintain maximum water quality, clarity, and carrying capacity.

Biological Filtration

Biological filtration is the most important cleansing process in ponds and other aquatic systems. It is carried out by specific bacteria, through the chemical processes of nitrification and denitrification. While they are also found suspended in the water, the majority of these bacteria grow in a film that covers the submerged surfaces of the pond.

Optimal water quality is essential to maintain a healthy environment for your koi.

The clarity of this pond is achieved through the use of a properly designed filtration system.

Understanding the Nitrogen Cycle

Nitrogen, the major component of air, is used by organisms for the synthesis of proteins and other compounds. Most organisms cannot use elemental nitrogen gas straight from the air, but rather must obtain it in a combined form. Various types of organisms are capable of using different kinds of nitrogen compounds. For example, animals generally obtain their nitrogen from the complex organic compounds known as proteins and amino acids; plants can utilize simple inorganic nitrate compounds; and various bacteria can make use of even simpler compounds such as nitrites and ammonia, which are toxic to plants and animals.

When organic matter decays, its proteins are broken down by bacteria. Among the products are ammonia. Ammonia is also released through a fish's gills as a metabolic waste product. The accumulation of ammonia in a closed system such as a pond is a serious problem as it is toxic to fish in low concentrations. Fortunately, once in the water, ammonia is utilized as an energy source by several types of *nitrifying* bacteria. *Nitrosomonas* chemically transforms ammonia into less toxic nitrites. Another species, *Nitrobacter*, utilizes the nitrites as an energy source, converting them into still less toxic nitrates. In this form they can be utilized by plants, which turn them back into protein. Some of the nitrate is converted by *denitrifying* bacteria into free nitrogen, which rises in bubbles to the top of the pond and is released back into the atmosphere.

While in a pond system the nitrification process occurs most intensively within the filter, the bacteria which mediate the nitrogen cycle are present in virtually every part of the pond, including plant surfaces, pond sides, and debris.

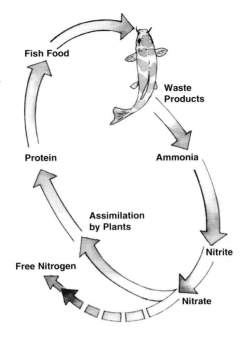

Biological filtration, accomplished through the nitrogen cycle, is principally carried out by bacteria in the filter bed.

Types of Biological Filters

Biological filters generally utilize sand and gravel layers as the filter media. Bacteria attach to the gravel grains and perform the necessary purification. It should be emphasized that the surface area of a filter is very important. The greater the surface area, the larger the population of nitrifying bacteria it can support, and the greater the *carrying capacity*, or the number of fish that can be maintained in the koi pond. For that reason alone, small submerged-type pond box filters sold for use in ponds are often inadequate as filters for a koi pond.

Although their actual appearance can vary according to the manufacturer or designer, filtration systems can be divided into two major types:

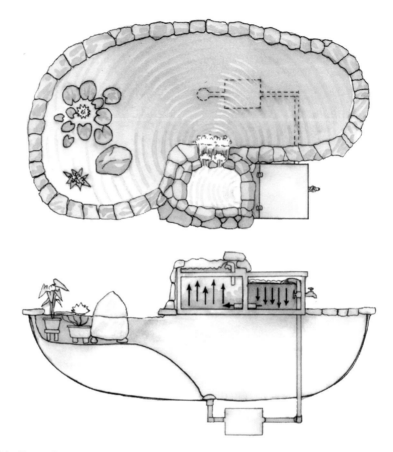

Filtration is important for the proper functioning of koi ponds. Biological filters can be located adjacent to the pond and concealed behind a waterfall or plantings. Care must be used in plumbing the filters to prevent leaks.

inside filters that are placed in the pond, and outside filters.

Though there are many designs, all operate in a similar manner.

Inside biological filters are often used in smaller ponds, and can be as simple as a small box holding filter media and a pump. Though they do a fair job of mechanical debris removal in smaller ponds, they are not as efficient as outside systems in providing optimal biological purification. Smaller filters perform best when the carrying capacity (or *bioload*) of the system is low.

The term *under-gravel filter* has been in common usage in the aquarium hobby to describe a type of sys-

tem that employs a perforated plate covered with gravel that rests on the aquarium bottom. The plate is connected to an inlet tube that is attached to a pump and an outlet tube from which filtered water is returned to circulation. Water is drawn through the plate, trapping debris, and bacteria remove ammonia from the water.

The major problem with such filters is that they clog easily. Also, koi are fond of rooting around in the filter bed, keeping the pond in a perpetually cloudy state. Therefore, if such a filter is used, an accessory mechanical filter will be required to remove debris. It is best to avoid this type of design unless you are planning to maintain a minimal amount of fish and use supplementary filtration methods.

Outside biological filters are the most popular systems. When designed correctly these can be very efficient and can be conveniently located perhaps concealed behind shrubs or trees. The filter is connected to the pond using a combination of intake and outlet pipes. Water is removed through a bottom drain and from several other areas of the pond, routed to the filter where it is purified, and returned to the pond through an aerating device such as a fountain or a waterfall. The filter can be either a gravity-fed or a reverse-flow type. Both can yield good results.

The advantage of outside filters is that they automatically remove debris and pollutants from the pond. Sediments and debris accumulate in the filter where they can then be removed through use of backwash systems (reversing the flow to remove trapped particles and debris). Such filters also are very easy to maintain. The surface of the filter need only be raked on occasion to break up the formation of algae. This prevents channeling. Finally, these filters are relatively easy to construct.

Selecting Filter Media

Selection of the proper shape and size of the gravel or other substrate is necessary for proper filter bed functioning. Size-graded gravel is the most common type of medium used in filter-beds. As most of the nitrifying activity is concentrated in the top layer of the filter, smaller-sized particles are used there to increase the available surface area. However, the grain size must not be so small as to prevent proper water circulation through the bed.

In outside biological filters, various types of gravel and rock should be layered. The total filter bed should be approximately 2 to 3 feet (61–91.4 cm) in depth. The topmost layer will be composed of fine gravel, gradually enlarging to large pebbles, small rocks, and large rocks. Generally, gravel grains of ⅛ to ¼ inch (3-6 mm) are recommended for the top layer. There should be an under-gravel substrate of at least 12 inches (30.5 cm) on the plate. Properly constructed, such a bed will allow proper percolation and backwashing of the filter.

Alternative substrates: With the advent of many new substrate materials, filter beds need not utilize only gravel. Some of these products actually perform better than the classical graded gravels. Filter bacteria are not fussy in their choice of surfaces to grow on. They will attach to gravel, plastic, epoxy, concrete, etc. Various

Biological filter beds should occasionally be raked to prevent clogging. Normal water flow through a clean filter is shown on the left; channeling and disruption of normal water flows as result of a clogged filter appears on the right. Clogged filter beds can develop anaerobic pockets that release toxic gases into the pond.

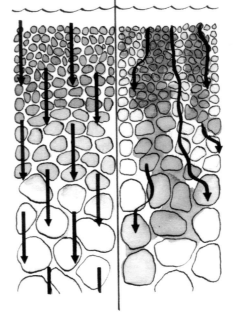

types of lightweight plastic and ceramic "biorings" have been marketed for some time. They provide plenty of surface area, but since they are relatively large they will not remove fine particles of debris as well as traditional layered-gravel filters. A secondary mechanical filter will be necessary.

Maintenance of the Filter Bed

If not overburdened, a properly designed biological filter bed is virtually maintenance free. Occasional backwashing and light raking of the surface is all that is necessary. Raking of the top of the filter bed retards the growth of algae, and avoids buildup of sediments and channeling.

Channeling can result when excessive amounts of debris plug the filter. Water then moves through zones of least resistance, forming channels, and leaving portions of the filter devoid of water circulation. This is a potentially dangerous situation.

Since the nitrification process is dependent on oxygen, the blocked areas begin to develop undesirable anaerobic bacteria that produce toxic gases such as methane and hydrogen sulfide, which can harm koi and other aquatic organisms.

A backwashing feature can be built into the system during its initial design. This is accomplished by the use of a pump that reverses the water-flow through a filter bed. In a gravity-flow filter the flow rate is controlled by a series of shut-off valves. The reverse action lifts the bed, releasing trapped materials, which can then be discharged into a waste-water outlet. Generally, backwashing once every three to four weeks is sufficient for most filter beds.

Conditioning

Like aquariums, ponds require conditioning after they are placed in operation. The conditioning period is the time required for nitrifying bacteria to become established on the filter bed of a new pond. Although other organisms are also establishing themselves during this time, it is the nitrifying bacteria that are the essential components of a biological filter.

New ponds undergoing conditioning have certain water characteristics, including high ammonia, the presence of nitrite, and a slow increase of nitrate. Once the conditioning period is over, ammonia and nitrite should not be detectable, although nitrate will continue to accumulate as the end product of nitrification.

It is important not to overstock the pond with fish during the conditioning period so as to minimize stress and possible koi mortalities. If the pond is overstocked, the concentration of toxic ammonia will increase, possibly to lethal levels.

The conditioning period requires approximately four to six weeks at temperatures of 75° to 80°F (24°–26.5°C). At the end of this period the filter bed should be stabilized with an ample supply of bacteria to purify the water properly.

Tip: To shorten the conditioning period, you can "seed" the new filter bed with several buckets of filter gravel from an established pond. This will introduce the nitrifying bacteria necessary to start the growth of the biological filter bed.

Tip: Under no circumstances should any medications or chemicals be added to the koi pond during the conditioning period. Some of these substances are known to either inhibit or prevent the development of filter-bed bacteria. Chemicals containing methylene blue or erythromycin particularly affect the growth of filter-bed bacteria adversely.

Filtration Rates

Water should flow through the filter at a rate that provides slightly more than adequate turnover. The filter size will obviously depend on the size of the pond as well as the rate at which the recirculating pump operates. A general rule of thumb is that water should have a minimum turnover rate through the filter of about 2 to 6 gallons (7.57–22.7 L) per square foot (.093 m^2) of filter surface per minute.

Of course, the rate will need to be adjusted according to the system. Always purchase a pump that allows variable adjustment of the circulation rate. As a general rule, the total volume of water should pass through at least one complete cycle in about two hours.

Carrying Capacity

Carrying capacity, or *bioload*, is the quantity of fish that a pond can safely sustain once the system has been conditioned. A common mistake is not allowing for the fact that koi grow very quickly. For example, small 3- to 4-inch (7.6–10.2 cm) koi will grow to be 12 inches (30.5 cm) or more within a few years. As they grow they add to the bioload, increasing the daily amount of ammonia and waste products added to the pond. At the point where the filter can no longer handle the waste products generated by the koi, you will either have to add additional filter capacity or reduce the number of koi to bring the pond back to its carrying capacity. Therefore, it is better to plan ahead by carefully considering the initial number of koi.

Various calculations can be used to determine the amount of fish to be added to your pond. One calculation involves the weight of fish per gallon, and others use pond surface area as a determination. This latter method makes a good rule of thumb, since it takes into consideration the increased oxygen requirements of the growing fish. The only difficulty, as with all rules of thumb, is that it assumes ideal conditions.

Add one 10-inch (25.4-cm) fish for every 20 square feet (1.86 m sq) of pond surface area. For example, a pond with dimensions of 10 x 20 feet (3.05 x 6.1 m) would be 200 square feet (18.6 m sq). With proper filtration and aeration, the pond could accommodate a maximum of 10 koi, each 10 inches (25.4 cm) long. One must bear in mind that this is a very conservative figure, and that to a pond that utilizes maximal filtration rates, aeration, water temperatures, frequent water changes, and proper feeding of the koi, additional fish could be added safely. On the other hand, ponds with marginal filtration, overfeeding, infrequent water changes, poor aeration, high water temperatures, and algal problems may not be able to sustain the recommended amount of healthy fish safely.

Mechanical Filtration

Mechanical filtration is the process of removing suspended particulate matter from water. This function is performed by the filter sand in which debris is trapped. The filter sand can either be inside or outside the pond. A problem with having an in-pond system is that koi like to root around in the gravel bed, stirring the debris back into the water, which creates turbidity.

Because excess accumulation plays a role in development of certain disease organisms, the reduction of particulate matter in koi ponds is extremely important. Particulate matter includes uneaten food, plant materials, fecal waste, and dead organisms. Eventually the material settles as sediment on the pond bottom, where it can be stirred up when disturbed by the fish.

Excessive buildup of these deposits promotes the development of certain protozoans that can attack the fish, such as *Epistylis* and *Vorticella*, and anaerobic bacteria, whose metabolic wastes are toxic to fish and plants.

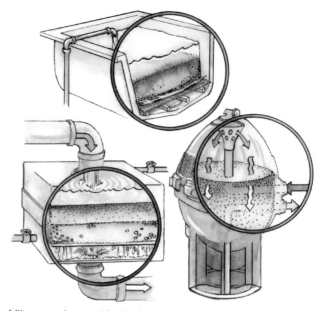

Various types of filters can be used for the koi pond: biological filters (top and left); sand pressure filters (right).

In many situations only a biological filter will be needed. In koi ponds with large numbers of koi, numerous plants, and low water movement, however, an accessory system is highly recommended to pre-filter particulate matter from the water prior to its passage through the biological filter bed.

Pressurized sand filters: For large koi ponds, the use of pressurized sand filters makes the job of removing suspended particles from the water easy. These are the same type of filters used to clarify swimming pools. They utilize fine sand as a substrate, have a high turnover rate, and are capable of efficiently removing particulate matter. Keep in mind that they are purely mechanical and perform little, if any, biological filtration.

Pressurized sand filters require some routine maintenance, and it is imperative that they be backwashed on a regular schedule. Some models have a built-in setting that will back-

wash automatically on a preset schedule. Generally, mechanical filters should not be used without additional biological filtration. To use such a system successfully the number of fish must be kept low, and the pond will need to be flushed regularly (or continuously) with fresh water to keep organics and debris at low concentrations.

Chemical Filtration

Chemical filtration is the removal of dissolved organic and inorganic compounds by adhesion onto porous substrates or by chemical processes such as air-stripping, ozonation, and ultraviolet light.

Various chemicals, originating from various biological activities, accumulate in water. These pollutants often give water a yellowish appearance. The chemicals in question include proteins, fats, amino acids, and other organics. Evidence continues to accumulate concerning the deleterious effects of some of these chemicals on fish. In the majority of cases removal is accomplished by making regular water changes each month and/or by the use of special substances such as activated carbon.

Activated carbon is an effective chemical filtrant that removes various pollutants as well as detergents and insecticides. Although the constant use of activated carbon is generally unnecessary in ponds, it can be employed when necessary to reduce the concentration of undesirable pollutants. It is particularly useful for removing medications and chemicals from water after treatment has been completed.

Various types of activated carbon are commercially available. Selected *liquid-phase*, granular-type carbons should be used for pond-water filtration. This is critical, as there are different types of carbons used for filtering air as well as water. Liquid-phase activated carbons will not remove oxygen, trace elements, ammonia, nitrites and nitrates. Consult your local garden shop or pond retailer for more information on selecting carbons for use in pond filters.

Zeolites are another group of naturally occurring materials that perform chemical filtration. These are able to remove ammonia from water. One pound (0.45 kg) of zeolite is capable of removing 0.5 grams of ammonia per day. Zeolite is useful for emergency situations, however their disadvantage is that they have a maximum limit for ammonia absorption. When left in the filter for extended periods, the substrate will eventually transform into a biological filter bed.

Zeolites (unlike activated charcoal) can be recharged. They must be removed and placed in a 10 percent salt solution, after which the zeolite is rinsed well with fresh water and placed back in the filter for reuse. Because of the occasional necessity for this inconvenient operation, zeolites are best used in temporary situations such as holding ponds, rather than as a permanent substrate in filters.

Ultraviolet sterilizers have been employed extensively in larger tropical aquarium systems, such as those used in public aquarium exhibits. They have not been used as extensively in ponds, but, depending on the size of your system, can be useful for optimizing water clarity. When set up properly they are capable of reducing the number of bacteria, parasites, and phytoplanktonic algae. As a general rule, they should be considered as optional equipment and not as a requirement for the successful operation of a koi pond. However, they can be useful to reduce parasites and algae. Efficacy of the UV systems depends on various factors including wattage of the bulbs, flow rate, and water turbidity.

Water Quality and Analysis

Once the pond is in operation, careful monitoring of water quality will be necessary. This chapter provides an overview of various water-quality parameters and how they help to provide a proper environment for koi.

Water-Quality Parameters

Several major changes come into play once the system is set into operation, including a rise in ammonia, nitrite and nitrate concentrations, an increase in phosphates, and a decline in pH.

These changes necessitate a program of regular water-quality monitoring of your koi pond. The diligent monitoring of water quality will ensure long-lived and healthy fish.

Temperature

Temperature tolerances vary according to the species of fish. Koi are a very hardy species, tolerant of temperature changes and fluctuations. Nevertheless, a range of 68° to 75°F (20.0°–23.9°C) is recommended, especially during the summer season. Gradual change from one temperature to another is also recommended.

Dissolved Oxygen

Oxygen that is dissolved in the the water (DO) is in great demand in koi ponds and other aquatic systems. It is consumed by fish and plants in respiration, and is utilized in various chemical processes, including bacterial decomposition in the nitrogen cycle. The amount of dissolved oxygen required is referred to as biological oxygen demand (BOD). The filter bed is a heavy user of oxygen.

The solubility of oxygen in water is dependent on several factors, including temperature, salinity, and agitation. In freshwater systems, the effect of salinity is negligible.

Temperature inversely affects oxygen solubility. The higher the temperature, the lower the DO level. As the oxygen concentration decreases below acceptable levels, koi will react with an increased respiratory rate. As a general rule, dissolved oxygen concentrations should be maintained at 5.0 to 5.5 mg per L, at least.

Low dissolved oxygen concentration is often a problem during summer months when water temperatures increase. Low oxygen concentration in koi ponds can also be traced to excess organic materials. Although koi are capable of tolerating low concentrations of oxygen for short periods, extended exposure can be dangerous.

Ample water circulation and agitation are critical in a koi pond. In ponds with poor water agitation, oxygen levels can quickly drop to abnormally low concentrations. The idea is to keep the water surface moving constantly so that oxygen is dissolved properly. The most common methods of agitation involve the use of rock raceways, waterfalls, and fountains. High turnover rates through filters also achieve the same result, keeping the dissolved oxygen level high. Maintaining oxygen at saturation is highly desirable.

It is important to note that koi will utilize more oxygen after feeding. If the fish are fed heavily at high water temperatures, the increased oxygen consumption can reduce oxygen levels to dangerously low concentrations.

Dissolved oxygen can also be depleted when heavy growths of algae occur. Algae produce oxygen during the day but utilize oxygen at night, and heavy growth can be a problem.

Carbon Dioxide

Carbon dioxide is a product of respiration by both plants and animals. In ponds it is dissolved in the water, from which it can be driven off by agitation. Just as low agitation can reduce the amount of dissolved oxygen, it also prevents the proper dispersion of carbon dioxide. High levels of carbon dioxide can severely affect normal respiration, preventing the intake of oxygen, even though ample oxygen may be present.

pH

Water can be acidic, neutral, or alkaline. The measure of this, referred to as pH, must be monitored regularly.

The pH of pond water increases naturally over time due to an increase in organic matter and a decrease in the buffering capacity of the water. Koi are quite tolerant of various pH levels. However, it is recommended that the pH not fluctuate too greatly, and not be lower that 6.8 or higher than 8.0. In general, koi prefer alkaline water, 7.0 to 7.8, with 6.8 and 8.0 being the upper and lower limits. Juvenile koi are more sensitive to pH changes than adults. Rapid changes in pH can result in shock.

If the pH is not within recommended ranges, it can be adjusted using commercially available buffers. These will either raise or lower the pH.

Tip: To prevent pH shock to koi, never attempt to adjust the pH of the pond water unless you have an

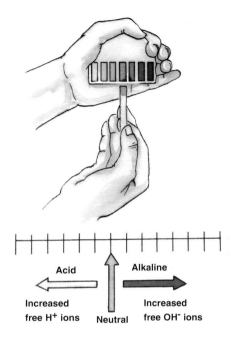

Acid — Increased free H^+ ions

Neutral

Alkaline — Increased free OH^- ions

Conducting routine water tests is an important means of ensuring that pond water stays within acceptable parameters. Tests are easy to perform using various types of commercial kits.

accurate pH test kit. And never attempt to alter the pH by more than 0.2 units a day.

Hardness

Hardness is defined as the amount of calcium and magnesium carbonate present in water. Hardness varies depending on the area of the country. Koi do poorly in extremely hard water, and will not survive in soft water. In addition, soft water has poor buffering capacity—that is to say, it lacks the ability to maintain a stable pH. Moderately hard and very hard conditions are generally associated with buffer compounds. Carbonates and bicarbonates decrease pH decline in pond water.

Hardness is generally expressed in degrees of carbonate hardness (DH) or parts per million (ppm). Water is considered soft if it has a hardness of less than 75 ppm, and hard if within 150 to 300 ppm.

Research has shown that various ions, such as calcium and magnesium, must be available in sufficient quantities not only for the survival of koi and other fish but for the proper functioning of the biological filter. In the absence of these ions, carbonates are not able to be used, and the water will become progressively acidic unless it is flushed or buffers are added on a routine basis.

Maintaining proper water hardness can be a serious problem. It should be monitored, especially in areas where the water is soft. Koi prefer moderately hard, alkaline water, in which they appear to have brighter colors.

Nitrogen Compounds

The accumulation of inorganic nitrogen in ponds can be quite troublesome for the new koi pond owner. Inorganic nitrogen includes ammonia, nitrite and nitrate. These are generated from the breakdown of organic materials. Accumulation of nitrogen compounds can predispose fish to diseases, reduce normal growth, and damage delicate gills.

Ammonia is the principal product of the decay of nitrogenous waste. Excreted by koi, principally through their gills as a waste product, it is, as discussed, the most toxic of the nitrogen compounds. Ammonia can be toxic to koi at low concentrations, and is especially so to fry and juvenile fish.

Ammonia readily dissolves in water and exists in two different forms: as toxic free ammonia (NH_3) and in the nontoxic ionized form, called ammonium (NH_4^+). The percentage of each type is dependent on a number of factors, including pH and temperature. High pH and temperature favor the toxic free-ammonia form. The tox-

icity of ammonia is dependent on various factors, including individual species sensitivity.

Koi are more tolerant of slightly higher concentrations of ammonia than many other fish species. The presence of toxic concentrations of ammonia in water interferes with the koi's ability to utilize oxygen normally. The condition can easily be mistaken for low-oxygen or high-carbon-dioxide levels.

Excessive concentration of ammonia is an indicator of inefficient biological filtration, overfeeding, overcrowding, and the decomposition of organic material in the pond. If the concentration is above acceptable levels, an immediate water change must be made to prevent mortalities. As a general rule, free ammonia should not exceed 0.036 mg per gallon (0.01 mg/L).

Nitrite, formed from the metabolic conversion of ammonia by *Nitrosomonas* bacteria, is the ionized form of nitrous acid. While it is less poisonous than ammonia, it is extremely dangerous to koi. High concentrations occur principally during the conditioning period of the biological filter. Typically, when this time is past, nitrite concentrations will be negligible. A continual persistent concentration of nitrite in the pond indicates a problem with the filter.

The toxicity of nitrite is due to its effects on oxygen transport, damage to important compounds in the blood, and direct damage to fish tissue. Like ammonia, it can affect the normal growth of koi, even when present in low concentrations.

Nitrates are formed from the oxidation of nitrites by bacteria. They are very soluble in water, and are much less toxic than ammonia or nitrite. In pond water, they could become a problem when present in concentrations in excess of 200 ppm (mg/L). Like nitrites, nitrates can affect the intake of oxygen by koi and reduce their normal growth rate.

Avoiding problems with nitrogen compounds: Nitrogen concentrations can increase quickly in systems with inadequate filtration. Biological filters must operate continuously to prevent accumulation of ammonia. Therefore, you should never shut off the biological filter for any length of time, especially during the warm summer months.

Other Toxic Chemicals

Other chemicals that are toxic to koi include chlorine and chloroamines, heavy metals, detergents, and insecticides. Caution must be used to prevent the introduction of such compounds into your pond. For example, care must be taken to ensure that insecticides are kept away from the pond. Covering the pond is the best safety measure if garden sprays need to be used in adjacent areas.

Chlorine and chloramine have been in common use for the disinfection of municipal water for many years. The concentrations of chlorine normally found in drinking water are extremely toxic to fish. Therefore all water, other than well water, must be treated with multipurpose water conditioners to remove any chlorine. When properly used, dechlorinating conditioners allow introduction of koi to the pond within the same day.

Chloramine can also be present in city water and has recently come into use in most American municipalities, with a continual switch from chlorine to chloramine over the past several years. This compound can be thought of simply as chlorine and ammonia combined. It is even more toxic than elemental chlorine. Tests have shown that as little as 0.05 ppm of chloramine can kill fish. Unlike chlorine-treated water, agitation of the water alone will not dissipate chloramine.

Water that contains chloramines must be treated prior to addition to the koi pond. Chloroamines can be detoxified in water by the addition of all-purpose commercial water conditioners that destroy chloramine. An alternative method is to filter water by passing it through activated carbon or an ammonia-reducing zeolite.

For most pond owners, the easiest way to detoxify chloramines is to add a water conditioner to the pond in the area where you add new water, but this method is suitable only when small amounts of water (less than 10 percent of the pond volume) are being replaced, such as in cases of partial water changes, or the replacement of evaporated water. You should note that when chloroamines are destroyed they release ammonia into the water. In ponds with inadequate filtration, a temporary rise in ammonia can occur. This should not be a problem in ponds with slightly acidic water and a well-functioning filter. In alkaline water, however, the ammonia remains in the toxic form. Nevertheless, in well-filtered ponds the ammonia will be rapidly destroyed by the biological-filter-bed bacteria. Consequently you need not be too concerned when making partial water changes to the pond, or when replenishing water lost by evaporation.

Tip: Call your local water company to see if chlorine or chloramine is used in your drinking water.

Heavy metals: Water can contain traces of copper, lead, aluminum, and zinc, metals that are toxic in low concentrations. Koi pond owners should be aware of the potential problems with these. Heavy metals can be present in city water as well as well water. Older plumbing can contribute substantial amounts of copper, lead, and zinc. Metals can exist in free or chelated form. The harder the water, the less toxic is the metal.

Copper can be found in water in low quantities, especially in summer periods, when it is used to control the growth of algae in reservoirs.

Freshwater fish are not very tolerant of copper, most fishes being sensitive to concentrations of 0.5 ppm or less. The toxicity of copper and other metals is dependent on several factors, including dissolved oxygen level, pH, temperature, and concentration of organics. The more alkaline the pH, the faster copper and other metal ions will precipitate out (chelate), thereby reducing toxicity.

Tip: Never use copper piping, fixtures, or equipment in koi ponds.

Water Analysis

The regular monitoring of water quality in the garden pond is an important part of preventative water maintenance. Some tests should be conducted on a weekly basis while others should be performed monthly.

The frequency of testing is dependent on various factors. Generally, the newer the pond the more frequently the tests should be performed. Once the pond has been conditioned and is in operation for several months, the frequency can be reduced to several times a month, unless you suspect a problem is developing. Once the pond has been in operation six to eight months, you will have gathered a baseline for your pond system. This will be valid as long as no major changes are made to the pond. However, if you add five new large koi to your pond, then you would increase the test frequency for ammonia, pH, nitrite and nitrate until you are assured that the additional animals have not substantially impacted on the stability of the pond ecosystem.

The purpose of regular water-quality testing is to detect any trends in water-deterioration before they reach a critical point. This enables you to make minor adjustments to restore the water quality to the baseline range. For example, if the pH of your pond is normally 7.0 to 7.2, and your water tests show that it has been declining over several weeks to 7.0, this would indicate that a water change is needed to restore the pH to the acceptable range.

Test Kits

Various types of water kits are readily available commercially. The most popular are colorimetric systems that rely on a change of color in the test sample. All colorimetric kits perform in a similar manner, but differ in their design depending on the manufacturer. Some provide powdered reagents, others are liquids, and still others come in tablet form. Dry reagents are for the most part more stable chemically than liquids.

The kits are relatively easy to use. Specific chemicals are added to a water sample. If the target chemical is present in the water a color change will be produced. The sample color is matched with a series of standards which indicate the approximate concentration of the particular parameter being tested.

The cost of the kits vary according to the particular test and the quality of the kit. Be sure to select a kit designed for use in aquatic systems with living animals.

Another possible approach is the "dipstick" method. Test strips are manufactured with chemicals impregnated on small pads of material. The strip is dipped in the water, allowed to develop color for several minutes or more, and the final color is compared to a chart. They are easy and fast to use; however, their limitation is that many only register within a broad range that does not provide enough accuracy for the purposes of a pond owner.

In addition to colorimetric kits, some parameters of water such as pH and dissolved oxygen can be tested using electronic laboratory instruments. Although more expensive than colorimetric kits, they are far more accurate in their determination of specific parameters. However, for most koi pond owners, this level of accuracy is unnecessary.

Selection of test kits involves the consideration of several key factors. These include the reputation of the manufacturer, accuracy, ingredient quality, reagent stability, ease of use, and cost per test. Comparing one test kit with another is not always easy. You should rely on the expertise of your garden and pond retailer to provide you with details on the advantages and disadvantages of one kit over another.

Tip: It is important to note that test kits designed for swimming pools, reflecting ponds, Jacuzzis, and spas are not appropriate for use in testing pond-water quality.

Troubleshooting Possible Water-Analysis Errors

Conducting water tests is relatively easy and in most situations is accurate. The instructions on each type of kit may vary depending on the manufacturer, but some general tips can be given here, in the event that difficulty is encountered when using them.

Various difficulties can arise when using commercial water-test kits, giving inaccurate results. Some of the most common reasons include too small a sample, chemical interference, using outdated chemicals, making errors in calculations, and contamination of the sample or the test chemicals.

It is important to follow instructions strictly on where to collect the sample and the proper sample size. If you are testing the koi pond for oxygen, for example, the recommended area for sample collection is away from the portion of the pond with the greatest water agitation. In addition, make sure that the sample you collect is clean and free from any debris. If the water is cloudy or contains sediment, collect another water sample or filter it before testing.

A colorimetric test kit (top) relies on a change of color in the test sample. The sample is then matched with a set of color standards to determine the concentration of the chemical being tested. Though more precise than a colorimetric kit, an electronic pH meter (center) is more expensive and requires more maintenance. Simple dip stick kits (bottom) are also available.

Contamination of the water sample and using outdated chemicals are two of the most common sources of water-test errors. It is extremely important, after completing each test, that the test vials be washed out thoroughly and air-dried. Glass or plastic vials should be cleaned after each use. Plastic vials can pose problems during cleaning as abrasive materials will scratch the surfaces of the test vial. Water and reacted test solution should never be left in the vial.

The use of multipurpose water conditioners has become virtually universal. Many, however, contain polymers that are known to interfere in water testing. Polymers such as polyvinylpyrolidone (PVP), found in many water conditioners, will give erroneous readings, indicating high concentrations of nitrogen compounds, including ammonia, nitrite and nitrate.

Be careful to avoid contamination when collecting water samples.

There is a potential problem in testing for nitrate in water, especially in new ponds. The majority of test kits for nitrite use a chemistry that converts nitrate to nitrite, which then reacts with another chemical that produces color in the test sample. If both nitrite and nitrate are present in the sample, the test will read both the nitrite and nitrate, giving an erroneously high nitrate reading. Therefore, prior to doing a nitrate test in your pond, first run a nitrite test. Record your results, then perform a nitrate test. Subtract the nitrite reading from the nitrate reading; this should give you a more accurate picture of the nitrate concentrations in your pond.

Chemical interference is widespread in water testing. The presence of chlorine in city water can oxidize the developing color in some tests, resulting in faded color and an inaccurate reading. That is why it is important to rinse vials with the water being tested prior to collecting the sample for a test.

Mathematical calculations must also be considered as possible sources of errors, as it is easy to make calculation errors. Nomenclature can also be a problem, as in the expression of nitrite as the ionic or nitrite-nitrogen form.

Contamination of one reagent by another is yet another problem. Droppers used for a given liquid chemical should never be used to dispense others. A tiny quantity of some chemicals can be sufficient to ruin an entire bottle of another.

Using chemicals that are old or outdated can cause errors. Those used for the detection of ammonia, nitrite and nitrate are particularly susceptible to deterioration. Always read the instructions on your kit regarding correct storage and handling of the chemicals supplied. All test kits should be stored at low temperatures to prevent chemical deterioration.

Pond Care and Maintenance

Maintenance

Once the koi pond is in operation it will be necessary to perform routine maintenance tasks on a regular schedule. Daily, weekly, monthly, and special spring and winter maintenance of the pond will ensure its continued beauty and quality, at the same time providing a healthy environment for your koi. Ignoring routine maintenance tasks can eventually lead to clogged filters, malfunction of poorly-cared-for equipment, or even disasters such as the sudden draining of the pond due to tears in the pond liner.

In addition to the tasks associated with the pond itself, you should also make a regular examination of your koi to ensure that they are in good health and not developing any serious disease problems. Generally, the best time to do this is during feeding.

Seasonal Care

Winter

Preparations for the winter season will vary according to geographical region. In colder climates, they will include removal of all organic materials and leaves from the pond. Any tropical plants, such as water lilies and water hyacinths, should be removed and stored indoors. In most areas koi can be left in the pond for the winter; however, where winters are severe they will need to be moved inside for the season. This will require setting up a temporary holding facility in a garage or basement.

One of the more serious problems in cold climates is reduced oxygen concentration during the winter, which can affect the survivability of your koi. It could become necessary to maintain some gas exchange and prevent the pond from freezing solid. Several courses of action are possible, including covering the pond with plastic sheeting, hay, or other materials. However, in areas with severe winters this is inadequate. Another possibility is the installation of a small pool heater, but this can be very expensive in areas with long winters. Finally, there are small, thermostatically-controlled de-icing heaters that float on the pond surface and maintain a small open area. However, as with heaters, the cost of operating these can get prohibitive.

It is recommended that you check with your local garden and pond center, koi breeder, or pet store for recommendations about winterizing your pond in your geographic region.

In temperate climates, very little need be done. Remove any leaves or debris as recommended above. The koi will go into a stage of hibernation as the water temperatures drop. Their frequency of feeding and the amount of food given will need to be reduced. As the temperature drops, the koi will tend to remain in deeper areas of the pond.

Spring

At the end of winter, various maintenance tasks should be completed to prepare the pond for the new season. These include a major inspection of the pond and related filter system, a general cleanup, and checking for any water run-off areas around the pond perimeter. In addition, the koi should be carefully examined for diseases that may make their appearance in the early spring. Finally, you may wish to set up quarantine facilities for acquisition of new koi, add algicides to the pond system, examine the water plants and repot them if needed, replenish your water-test chemicals, and perform a set of water tests.

Prior to performing the tests, make sure that the chemicals you are using are not outdated. Test chemicals often have a limited shelf life and need to be replaced on a timely basis. Perform a standard set of tests, including pH, ammonia, nitrite and nitrate. If the pH is low, you will need to make the necessary water changes to bring the pH back to an acceptable level.

Checking the Pond and Equipment

One of the most important tasks is the inspection of the pond filters, including pipe joints and circulation pumps. Ponds with biological filters should be thoroughly checked by examining all fittings, pipes, and connections, to ensure that they are tight and don't leak. Faulty or cracked pipes need to be replaced.

Recirculation pumps need to be checked for corrosion. Dismantling of the pump to inspect the mechanism inside is recommended if you suspect a potential problem.

The filter bed should also be checked to ascertain whether it requires a thorough cleaning. The bed should be checked for clogging. Ponds that are equipped with a rapid sand-pressure filter should be thoroughly inspected and the filter sand replaced if necessary.

The pond itself should also be inspected thoroughly. Plastic-lined pools need to be checked for tears, abrasions, or leaking areas to determine if a replacement liner will be needed for the current season. Polyvinyl chloride (PVC) pool liners last longer than other material types, are stronger, have greater elasticity, and tend to crack less. In general, pond liners will last two to five years, depending on various factors including material composition, thickness, and the climate in the region where they are installed.

Fiberglass pools are quite durable, and generally will not require as extensive an examination as plastic-liner pools. Concrete pools will need to be examined closely to check for cracks. If cracks are found the pool will need to be drained completely and thoroughly cleaned prior to any repair work.

If soil and leaves have accumulated on the pond bottom in excess of 1 inch (2.54 cm), it will be necessary to drain the pond and remove this debris. Such a situation is potentially dangerous, since the thick sediment promotes the growth of anaerobic bacteria.

Examining Your Koi

Various diseases, especially those of bacterial origin, can make their appearance in the spring. Failure to recognize diseases early in their course can result in fatalities. This possibility is increased if koi were introduced to the pond in the fall. There are a number of reasons why diseases are more likely in spring.

Koi, like other fish, are cold-blooded animals. Their body temperature is close to the ambient water temperature. The functioning of the fish's immune system is related to temperature. During the winter a koi's physiological function changes dramatically. Respiration decreases, digestion ceases, and the immune system is for the most part nonfunctional.

64

In the spring, as water temperatures begin to increase, so does the fish's metabolism. The immune system, however, takes longer to become fully functional.

If koi were carrying a bacterial disease, for example, and were introduced to the pond in the fall, the low seasonal temperature would usually inhibit the development of the disease until spring. At that time, the fish will often be unable to fight the infection, since its immune system is not functioning at its capacity.

Also, as the water temperature increases bacteria in the water are able to grow faster, while the fish's immune system is still depressed. It may become necessary to treat the fish with antibiotics early in the spring as a preventive measure against development of bacterial disease. This will be discussed further in the chapter on diseases (see page 80).

Examination is best accomplished just prior to feedings, when the fish gather at the feeding area. Several aspects of their general behavior should be examined. Carefully evaluate their swimming abilities and respiration rate. See if they are scratching themselves on the pond bottom or staying in areas of high water agitation. Also evaluate their buoyancy, an aspect that is often affected if the fish begins to develop a systemic bacterial disease.

Next, look for any lesions, including frayed fins, ulcers, abnormal swellings, spots, etc. These could indicate developing bacterial or parasitic disease. The appearance of any transparent fecal casts in the water is a sign of possible bacterial, viral, or parasitic infections of the gastrointestinal tract.

Regular pond maintenance is required to keep ponds in the best condition. This large pond located in the Japanese Friendship Gardens in San Jose, California receives a thorough spring cleaning to remove accumulated sediments, as well as to prepare for inspection of the concrete surfaces to detect areas needing repair.

HOW-TO:
Pond Cleaning

Equipment

Some basic equipment will need to be acquired in order to perform the basic maintenance chores. This will include several clean buckets, a good-quality fishnet, and a dipping net for skimming off leaves and other debris. A barrier net is also recommended to easily herd koi for removal to temporary holding facilities. A hard bristle bush with a long handle is necessary for scrubbing the pond bottom and sides to remove excess algae, and a hose-powered pool vacuum cleaner is also helpful for removing debris from the bottom.

Caution: Care must be exercised when cleaning ponds with plastic liners. Hard bristles could damage the surfaces. Brushes with soft bristles are therefore recommended.

Removal of Organic Materials

Leaves from surrounding trees or shrubs that have fallen

Proper pond maintenance requires basic equipment including brushes, dip nets, holding containers, buckets, and a pool vacuum cleaner for larger ponds.

into the pond should be removed on a regular basis. Decaying leaves produce ammonia that can fuel the growth of unwanted algae. Leaves and other debris should be removed daily, particularly during the fall season. The severity of this problem is variable, depending on the region in which you live and the types of vegetation adjacent to the pond. Both leaves and evergreen needles decay in pond water, lowering the pH and, in the case of needles, releasing resins that are potentially harmful to koi. High water temperatures accelerate the decay process.

Removal of residual floating food: Any koi food remaining in the pond 1 hour after feeding should be removed using a dip net. If left in the pond, it will decay, contributing to the fouling of the pond water. This is far more serious in smaller koi ponds than larger ones.

Removal of Debris From Skimmers

Larger ponds often have overflow setups, or *skimmers*, that collect floating debris and other materials. If your pond has this feature, make sure that the overflow is cleaned daily in the summer and at least weekly during other seasons. The frequency of cleaning is based on prevailing water temperatures and how fast the overflows become filled with debris.

Cleaning of Recirculation and Submersible Pumps

Pumps should be inspected regularly, especially during the summer, to make sure they are functioning properly. Both types

Regular removal of debris from the pond is an important part of daily maintenance.

of pumps will generally require only cleaning of the strainer that traps large particles. The frequency of cleaning depends on your filtration system and water quality. You should check the manufacturer's recommendations on maintenance and service of your pond pumps.

Cleaning Filters

Although there are various types of filters, all will require some maintenance to assure their proper functioning. Sand pressure filters will require backwashing. Small submerged pond filters will need to be cleaned and any activated carbon or other filter materials changed.

Large biological filters will require regular maintenance. It is important to rake the surface of the filter bed every few days, especially in the summer months, to break up any algae growth and to minimize clogging and channeling. Clogged filters function at reduced efficiency, promoting the development of anaerobic bacteria and their toxic waste products.

A garden rake is all that is necessary to perform this maintenance task. Simply draw the rake across the top of the filter surface bed to break up the formation of any clumps of algae. Make sure the rake penetrates the surface to a depth of at least an inch or more.

Cleaning Excessive Algae

If excessive benthic algae has grown on the pond surfaces, remove it with a brush. This is not to imply that all algae should be removed, as it serves as food for koi. However, in order to maintain an aesthetic-looking pond, some algae can be removed from the surfaces. How often this is done is variable, depending on the season and geographical location. This task is required more often in ponds with inadequate filtration.

Changing Water

Once a month some water should be changed in the pond to reduce the build-up of nutri-

A common garden rake is useful for breaking up algal growths on the surface of biological filter beds.

ents. Although filters detoxify harmful nitrogen products such as ammonia and nitrite, other chemical components such as nitrate and various organics will remain in the pond water. A recommended solution to this problem is to make partial water changes to the pond to dilute these organics. The amount changed and the frequency depends on several factors. Generally, one-quarter of the volume should be changed once a month. In areas of the country where water conservation measures are in effect, you may not be able to do this that often. In this situation, it is recommended that you change one-third of the volume once every three months. The information you get from water tests will help guide you in setting a schedule for water changes.

Full Pond Cleaning

Every few years the pond will require a full cleaning. This will depend on the condition of the pond, filter type, and other factors. Full cleaning requires a complete draining of the water. Of course, the koi will have to be removed to a temporary holding area during cleaning and inspection.

Prior to the actual draining of the water, it is important to determine the amount and extent of any debris, such as leaves and sediment, on the pond bottom. If large amounts of debris are present, caution must be used to prevent disturbing the material while the koi are present in the pond. Disturbance of accumulated bottom materials releases toxic substances, reducing the concentration of

A barrier type net makes it easy to herd koi into sections of the pond for removal during cleaning operations.

dissolved oxygen. This reaction occurs quickly, especially in water with high temperatures.

To move your koi safely prior to draining and cleaning of your pond, it is recommended that you use a barrier-type net, with attached weights on one end and large enough to stretch across the full length of the pond. The koi can then be slowly herded into one section of the pond and removed using a dip net and a plastic tub. After removal, the koi should be placed in a holding facility with ample room, aeration, and a cover to prevent the fish from jumping out.

Once the koi are removed you can proceed to the cleaning. All water should be drained and the bottom sediment removed. If your pond has a drain installed, draining will be relatively simple. If not, a portable pump must be used to carry the water to a drain or to some other area away from the pond.

If there is a plastic liner it should be carefully inspected for any tears. Inspect concrete ponds for cracks in the pond bottom and sides.

Nutrition

Nutritional Guidelines

Extensive research has yielded a substantial amount of information about the nutritional requirements of koi. Although pond fish will accept just about any type of food offered, this should not be taken to mean that any type of food is necessarily good for them. There are clear nutritional guidelines which, if followed, will produce healthy, happy fish.

Nutrition and Disease

Lack of essential nutrients is known to have deleterious effects on the immune system. Koi with impaired immune systems are unable to fight infections properly. Deficiency or excess of certain nutrients can produce noninfectious diseases as well. Providing a good nutritional program, with the selection of properly formulated foods, is essential for healthy koi.

Metabolic Requirements

The nutrients supplied in the daily diet are utilized for various bodily functions. Koi energy requirements are variable, and depend on various factors including the age of the fish, its feeding habits, behavior, and water temperatures. Nutrients are used for growth, tissue repair, daily activity, and other functions as well. Koi will have different energy requirements depending on the stage of their life cycle as well. Younger koi need more calories per day to sustain their rapid growth and higher metabolic needs.

Some of the nutritional components in food are used for the production of energy, while others serve different purposes. Carbohydrates and fats are utilized for energy, while vitamins and minerals are needed for various life processes, from growth and tissue repair to nervous and glandular activity. Protein can serve many purposes, from energy to growth.

Koi Digestion

Many pond owners assume, when observing koi, that they simply gulp the food from the surface and swallow. This, however, is not the case. Koi lack teeth in their jaws, but do have molar-like *pharyngeal teeth* located in the throat. Food is first ground on a hard pad in the pharynx. This prepares the food for the digestive process.

Unlike some other fish, koi (and goldfish) lack true stomachs. The rate of digestion is variable, depending on several factors including water temperature, digestibility of the food, and age and size of the fish.

General Dietary Requirements

Koi require specific amounts of certain components in their diet. The major nutritional groups are protein, lipids (fats), carbohydrates, fiber, and vitamins and minerals.

Protein

Required for normal physiological function and growth, protein is found in plants, animals, and bacteria. The percentage of protein required varies according to species and age. Generally, the amount of protein in a diet can be reduced as the fish matures. For example, fry and finger-

Providing pond koi with the correct type and quantity of foods ensures their continued health and vibrant color.

ling koi should be fed diets which range from 37 to 42 percent protein. With adults, however, protein can be reduced to 28 to 32 percent. Under no circumstances should koi be fed a steady diet containing less than 28 percent protein, as deficiency will result.

Proteins are composed of smaller units called amino acids. There are 20 amino acids in all, and it has been determined that 10 of them are essential for normal growth and development. A deficiency in any of these essential amino acids results in low weight gain and depressed appetite. Some commercial diets, formulated solely from plant materials, are deficient in some essential amino acids.

Tip: "The more protein the better" is a poor standard for evaluating the quality of a food. Properly formulated foods should be designed to conform with the life stage of the fish and its appropriate protein requirements.

Lipids

Primarily an energy source, lipids are also a vital component of internal organs and cells. The high lipid content of fish helps them to maintain neutral buoyancy. Collectively, lipids include fats, phospholipids, steroids, and waxes.

Lipids are divided into two chemical categories—saturated and unsaturated. Unsaturates are more easily utilized than the saturates. In fact, too much saturated fat in the diet can have deleterious effects. Therefore, prepared diets that include saturated-fat sources such as pork, beef, or poultry should not be used for feeding koi. Such fats eventually deposit in the internal organs of the fish, causing metabolic dysfunction. On the other hand, diets high in unsaturated fish oils are preferred and are better utilized by koi. Most prepared diets have an acceptable 5 to 8 percent of total fat.

Avoid overfeeding your koi. Provide a small amount of pellets at first and make sure that the fish consume them completely before adding more pellets. Overfeeding can cause a buildup of food particles, which fall into the pond bottom, decay, and produce toxic ammonia.

Too much fat in the diet results in excessive weight gain and fatty infiltration of the liver. A deficiency in the essential fatty acids can cause fin erosion, predisposition to shock, and heart degeneration.

It is important that the foods fed to koi should be specially formulated for them. Some koi owners feed their fish pelleted catfish or salmon foods. This is not recommended, as such formulations often contain fats incompatible with the koi digestive system.

Carbohydrates

The majority of prepared foods, such as floating koi pellets, often contain high percentages of carbohydrates. In reviewing the ingredients in these foods you will notice they include various sources of carbohydrates, including wheat, corn, and rice.

In koi and many other fish species, carbohydrates are absorbed slowly as simple sugars. Although koi can utilize carbohydrates, recent research has indicated that they do not digest them as efficiently as once thought. Therefore, diets prepared primarily with cereals (rice, wheat, corn, etc.) should be avoided.

Fiber

Fiber is the diet component that is not digested during passage through the fish's intestinal tract. It is believed that fiber aids in digestion and the transit of food through the intestine. Although fiber is a necessary dietary component, excessive amounts can interfere with the absorption of various nutrients. Also, the excreted excess can significantly add to the organic debris in the pond. For these reasons high-fiber diets should be avoided. Prepared foods with fiber content below 5 percent are generally acceptable.

Vitamins

Important for various body functions, vitamins fall into two groups, those soluble in water and those soluble in fat.

Water-soluble vitamins include the B complex and vitamin C. The fat-soluble vitamins are A, D, E, and K. The requirements for vitamins in koi are variable, depending on numerous factors including age, size, stress, and prevailing water conditions. Vitamin deficiencies can be particularly serious in young fish.

Vitamin deficiencies result in various disease syndromes. The signs are often nonspecific, but generally a decrease in food consumption is noticed, with a developing pattern of increased mortalities. For example, when diets deficient in vitamin A are fed to koi they develop edema, exophthalmos (eye protrusion), and show decreased growth.

A deficiency of vitamin C results in scoliosis and bone malformation. C is one of the most important vitamins required for normal metabolic function. Koi are able to synthesize their own vitamin C; however, the amount made is generally inadequate for daily requirements. Hence, supplementary vitamin C should be provided in the diet. Many prepared koi foods include additional doses of this vitamin as supplements. High-quality koi foods now contain a new form of stabilized vitamin C that resists breakdown during extended storage.

Minerals

Minerals are required by koi for normal tissue formation, normal metabolism, and osmoregulation. (i.e., the various physiological processes that maintain the proper balance of salts and water within the fish). Fish obtain their minerals both from their food and directly from the water; however, only a few minerals can be absorbed in sufficient quantities from water. Iron, copper, iodine, magnesium, and others must be supplied in the diet.

Calcium and phosphorus are two important minerals required in large concentrations for normal growth and metabolic function. Koi are able to absorb calcium directly from the water, but they must have adequate concentrations of phosphorus in their diet to absorb the calcium.

A deficiency in dietary phosphate results in slower growth, appetite depression, and the development of deformed heads and backs.

Types of Koi Food

Food Types

Koi are omnivorous fish, consuming both animal and plant materials. Various types of food will be accepted by them, including fresh, freeze-dried, and dried preparations. Careful selection of various foods from these categories will ensure a healthy dietary regime.

Fresh food: Fresh vegetables including lettuce, squash, and others can be fed, but should be considered only as supplementary. Vegetables are best blanched in hot water, then cooled prior to feeding them to your koi. Pieces of shrimp, fish, earthworms, and clams are also acceptable as supplements and to supply some variety, but are not required foodstuffs.

Freeze-dried food such as plankton, fresh water shrimp, daphnia, and tubifex and bloodworms are sometimes used as supplements for feeding koi. Many of these are excellent sources of pigment, especially shrimp.

Prepared foods are very popular for feeding koi. They are available as sinking or floating pellets, as well as flakes. There are numerous formulations such as maintenance pellets, color diets, vegetable diets, wheat germ, and others. While the nutritional claims of many formulations are accurate, you should scrutinize the label ingredients carefully. Many of the inexpensive commercial formulations are virtually identical in the types of ingredients they use, and for all practical and nutritional purposes are interchangeable.

Pelleted foods are sold in a variety of shapes and sizes, either floating or sinking. Koi show little preference as to the shape of the food and will consume either stick or pellet formulations. There is no scientific evidence to suggest that one shape is better than another. Acceptance of foods by koi is related to the nutritional profile and ingredients used rather than their shape.

Since much of the enjoyment of your koi is seeing them feed at the surface, floating foods are recommended. Floating pellets also have the advantage in that you can determine if you are overfeeding, as with sinking pellets it is often difficult to assess whether all the food fed has

Various live foods are suitable for feeding juvenile koi including (clockwise from the top) daphnia, blood worms, brine shrimp, and cyclops.

been consumed. If food remains on the pond bottom too long it will decay, contributing to deterioration of the pond-water quality. Sinking pelleted foods are useful, however, if you have bottom-feeder fish in the pond in addition to your koi.

Evaluating Commercial Diets

Although there are numerous commercial feed formulations available on the market, not all are suitable for koi. From a scientific standpoint, diets range from those that are hazardous for use in feeding fish to high-quality formulations that conform to scientific standards.

The quality of commercial foods vary. You should be careful to purchase only those that are formulated specifically for feeding koi. There are many available and they come in various sizes for feeding small or large fish.

Various criteria are employed in the evaluation of commercial formulas. As discussed above, certain percentages of protein, fat, fiber, minerals, and vitamins must be present to constitute a quality diet. Many formulations contain excess protein. The only result of this is an increased nitrogen load in the pond water. Other formulations, on the other hand, have such a low percentage of protein as to be totally unsuitable for the normal growth of both juvenile and subadult koi.

Many of the "stick type" foods are full of air, have a questionable nutritional profile, and do not provide adequate nutrition. These foods are often incapable of meeting the caloric requirements of koi, especially juveniles. You must evaluate the data on the labels carefully prior to purchasing the food.

Feeding for Good Color

The Japanese term *ironage* (ee-ro-na-gay) indicates the process of maximizing the color of koi. The development of good color is based on two major factors: the genetic color potential of the fish and the type of diet given. The appearance of the color can be affected by water quality as well. If the water temperature is higher than recommended for koi, the colors can appear to have a "bleached out" appearance. Simply reducing the water temperature can restore a more natural appearance to the fish.

Not all koi have the genetic potential to develop maximum color brilliance, as this is more directly related to the type and concentration of skin pigments. Often young fish have good pigmentation, but as they mature their pigmentation changes, sometimes improving and other times becoming worse. This underlines the importance of carefully selecting quality koi from reputable suppliers.

It is desirable for the pond owner to understand what factors affect color in

A Grand Champion kohaku with excellent color and patterns. Good color in koi is genetically determined, but diet plays an important role in maintaining it.

koi. Color can be maximized by specific components provided in the diet. It is not enough to add some ingredient to the diet, the quantity as well must be within acceptable amounts.

Naturally occurring pigments are found in various ingredients used for formulating prepared diets for koi. For example, examine the list of ingredients on the label of a container of koi food pellets. Look for items such as shrimp meal, plankton, marigold petals, chlorella, and spirulina. Each of these is a source of pigments that can enhance the color of koi.

Spirulina in particular has become a popular ingredient in foods due to its superior ability to enhance koi color. It is a fresh water blue-green algae of worldwide distribution. It is renowned for its high protein and vitamin content, and also possesses a high concentration of pigments, especially *beta-carotene*. As many koi breeders are aware, the inclusion of spirulina in the diet will particularly enhance red, orange, and yellow colors in koi.

Freeze-dried foods, especially plankton, daphnia, and brine shrimp, contain high concentrations of compounds called *carotenoids*, a major pigment in the skin of koi.

Pigments can also be added to koi foods by using purified and concentrated substances, either natural or synthetic. One of the most widespread pigments used is *canthaxanthin*. When added to the diet in specific concentrations it will greatly enhance the red color of koi. Beta-carotene is also commonly added to prepared diets for color enhancement.

Finally, it should be noted that koi can be fed too many pigments in the diet, and this can alter the desired color of the koi. For example, in koi with a predominance of white on the body, too much carotenoids will have a tendency to cause some of the white areas to develop a pinkish cast. If this occurs, simply reduce the amount of color foods given, or switch to another diet. The overfeeding of diets high in spirulina is known to cause this condition.

Tip: Store all foods, especially color foods, in cool areas, since the majority of color pigments are easily destroyed by heat. Prepared foods containing high amounts of pigments should be stabilized with some type of antioxidant. *Ethoxyquin* is a common antioxidant added to fish diets, and is known to effectively prevent the destruction of pigments during storage.

Feeding Procedures

Fish should be fed several times a day, preferably in early morning, midafternoon, and late afternoon. Although it is popular to feed fish only during the morning and afternoon, recent study of koi digestion has indicated that they should be fed more frequently and in smaller amounts. When fed in this manner they are able to utilize carbohydrates more efficiently.

Young fish should be fed more often than adult fish. Newly acquired fish will need some behavioral training if you wish them to come to a specific area during feeding time. You should select one area in which to feed them. Once they are accustomed to this, they will congregate there, ready to be fed.

The amount of food given on a daily basis depends on numerous factors, including age, water temperature, and food quality. For good health and growth, they should receive 1 to 4 percent of their body weight per feeding. The upper figure is applicable to young growing koi. In practice, it is unnecessary to attempt such calculations, rather it is recommended to feed small amounts and to observe the koi carefully over time. Adjust the amount of food according to growth rate and overall appearance.

The determination of the actual amount to be given is extremely diffi-cult, and depends on various factors including the water temperature, number of koi, and their age. Care must also be exercised to prevent overfeeding, as koi can be gluttonous. Any excess food must be removed from the pond if it is not consumed within 20 minutes. By that time, uneaten food has lost many important nutrients, especially vitamins, to leaching.

Make sure all of the fish are receiving some food by scattering it in slightly different, but adjacent areas. This method is recommended to prevent larger fish from consuming larger quantities of food and preventing slower, smaller fish from eating.

Water temperature must also be considered when feeding. Koi consume more food in warmer water than in cooler. The amount of food should therefore be adjusted according to seasonal water temperatures.

Feeding in Autumn and Winter

The amount of food required for your koi will change as the water temperatures begin to decrease during the autumn and winter. In regions with cold temperatures, fish will cease eating completely for the winter. In temperate areas, they will simply reduce the amount and frequency of their food intake.

Well-balanced diets fed to koi during the growing season prepare them for the winter. Many hobbyists switch from maintenance diets to diets formulated with wheat germ. Although this has been popular in practice, there is insufficient scientific evidence to suggest that wheat germ makes any significant difference for overwintering.

Tip: The key point is to reduce the protein in the diet and to increase carbohydrates and fat slightly to promote fat storage for utilization during cold weather. If the fish are fed a balanced, high-quality diet throughout the growing season, they will naturally begin to

Various types of prepared foods are available commercially for feeding koi (clockwise from the top): flake foods, extruded stick foods, and floating pellets.

accumulate fat stores in preparation for the winter season.

As water temperatures decline, decrease the amount of food you feed to your koi. Do not abruptly cease feeding, but carefully observe the fish's behavior and continue to feed until they cease to show interest. You will see reduced feeding activity when the temperature dips below 50°F (10°C). Do not continue feeding at that point.

Feeding in Spring and Summer

As the winter season ends and spring arrives, profound changes occur in the fish's physiology. Caution should be used in offering too much food at the beginning of the growing season. Bear in mind that the koi's digestive system, including secretion of enzymes, has been virtually shut down throughout the winter, especially in those fish overwintered in colder regions.

The best approach is to start feeding small amounts once the water temperature has reached 60°F (15.5°C). Begin feeding once a day, then slowly increase the amount of food as the water warms. Avoid giving too much food to your koi. Rely on careful observations of the koi's behavior. It is better to underfeed than to overfeed.

It should be pointed out that overfeeding of prepared dry foods in colder water in the spring can sometimes induce intestinal blockage. Affected koi will exhibit several signs, most of which are quite obvious. First, the fish will appear to have difficulty in swimming. This is most often related to a buoyancy problem. Second, the fish will develop abdomi-nal distention, due to the accumulation of fluids in the abdominal cavity. It is important to note, however, that these signs are similar to those caused by bacterial infections and other disease agents. Therefore, it is easy to misdiagnose the problem. Generally, if you have not overfed your koi, more than likely the problem is related to an infectious organism.

Food Storage

Foods must be properly stored away from heat and moisture to preserve their quality. Leaving bags of flakes or pellets open to the air causes deterioration. Toxic substances can be produced by the growth of microbial contaminants, fat oxidation, and growth of molds and other organisms. Infestation by insects, including ants and weevils, can easily occur.

Vitamins are particularly susceptible to deterioration. For example, vitamin C is very sensitive to heat. Within three months, food stored under high humidity and temperatures of approximately 79°F (26.1°C) or more will lose a minimum of 50 percent of its initial vitamin C content. Vitamin B_6 (pyridoxine) and B_2 (riboflavin) are also susceptible to rapid nutrient destruction during extended storage.

Dry prepared foods must be stored in cool, dry conditions. It is recommended that 90 days be the maximum storage time for foods stored at room temperatures. If you are going to need to store larger amounts of food for longer periods, it is recommended that they be packed in double plastic bags or in recloseable plastic containers and stored in a freezer.

Quarantine

Quarantine prevents the inadvertent transmission of various infectious diseases. Even though fish appear to be in good health, they may be carriers of disease agents, including parasites, bacteria, and viruses. Common parasites, especially flukes, anchorworms, fish lice, and protozoans such as ich are easily transmitted from infected koi to other fish in the pond. Quarantine procedures should always be followed carefully to achieve the best results.

Fish That Should Be Quarantined

It is important not to overstock the pond during the first four to six weeks, as it takes that much time to condition the biological filter. It is also necessary to perform the water tests for ammonia, nitrite, nitrate, and pH every few days for the first several weeks to ensure that the values do not reach toxic levels. The first group of fish should be quarantined if at all possible before their introduction to the pond. There are several reasons why this is especially important. If the new fish are carrying a disease, it could necessitate treatment of the pond system. As previously noted, the necessary chemicals and antibiotics could affect the biological filter bacteria and damage plants.

Any new koi that you purchase thereafter will also need to be quarantined. Even if the fish you purchase have gone through a quarantine period, you should still place them in your own quarantine tank as a safety measure.

Fish entered in a competition should be quarantined prior to reintroduction to your pond. There is no other way to guarantee that disease agents are not inadvertantly carried home from the exhibition tanks.

The Quarantine Tank

You must have the quarantine tank ready and conditioned prior to the addition of any fish. The container must be used exclusively for quarantine and treatment purposes. Various containers are suitable for quarantine, including large aquariums and fiberglass holding tanks. For quarantining smaller juvenile fish, a tank of 50 to 125 gallons (189–473 L) should be ample. For quarantining larger koi, 10 inches (25 cm) or more, the quarantine tank should be at least 150 to 250 gallons (568–946 L).

Important: Never crowd too many fish in the quarantine tank as this will additionally stress the fish.

Locating and Equipping the Quarantine Tank

The isolation tank should be located in an area away from the main pond and out of direct sunlight. It should be equipped with a biological filter and, in most cases, a heater. Providing aeration is important to ensure good water circulation, proper gas exchange, and high dissolved oxygen levels.

The heater will maintain a constant temperature in the tank, which is critical while treating fish during quarantine. Heaters are available in various wattages depending on the size of the container. For quarantine tanks they are available in sizes from 100 watts up. A rule of thumb is 2 watts per gallon (3.8 L) of water to be heated.

New koi should be carefully examined upon acquisition and placed in quarantine facilities. Check the body for the presence of any lesions or parasites.

All quarantine tanks should be covered to prevent the koi from jumping out. Choose a cover that permits you to observe the koi easily. A wooden frame with plastic web netting is simple to construct.

When not in active use, the quarantine tank can be kept operating to keep the biological filter functioning. Should you decide to follow this procedure, the tank should not be used again for six to eight weeks. Alternatively, it can be dismantled and sterilized between operations.

Receiving New Koi

With newly acquired koi, check the pH and water temperature of the quarantine tank, and verify that the filter is functioning properly.

Place the box with the koi in a shaded area. It is important to open the lid of the styrofoam box slowly and in dim light so as not to stress the fish any further. If the box is opened in sunlight the fish will become frightened and may begin to jump.

Before adding the fish to the quarantine tank make sure the water temperature in the tank is close to the temperature of the water in the shipping bag. Place the container in the quarantine tank and allow the two water temperatures to equilibrate. Normally, if the koi are being moved from cooler water to slightly warmer water, there is less chance of thermal shock.

When everything is ready, place the shipping bag into the tank water, open it, and gently tip the fish into the water. Carefully guide them from the bag into the tank, at the same time minimizing the amount of water spilling over into the tank from the shipping bag. In some cases, if the koi are small enough you can reach into the bag and lift the koi out. The use of a net is not recommended, since this can injure their skin.

Cover the tank securely with a screen top to prevent the fish from jumping out. Start the quarantine period procedure as previously outlined.

After the fish have been released and have acclimated for several hours, try to examine them. Because any physical injury can invite infection by bacteria or fungi, it may be necessary to institute some type of treatment immediately.

In examining the koi, ask yourself a series of questions. Are there any skin lesions, raised scales, open wounds, or frayed fins? Is labored respiration evident? Frequent or occasional scratching? Are any white spots present on the body? Are the eyes protruding or turbid? Is there a general white or gray cloudiness to the skin? Any tumorlike growths? These signs are useful in making a diagnosis. For example, frequent scratching and heavy respiration could indicate external parasites such as flukes. Protruding eyes could indicate a systemic bacterial infection.

Koi should be permitted to acclimate to the quarantine conditions for 24 to

48 hours before administration of any medications. The exception is the use of antibiotics, which will be necessary if lesions are noticed on the body. Fish can be fed sparingly during the initial 48-hour period if they show interest.

Treating the Fish

Quarantine Period
A quarantine period of 14 to 21 days is recommended for all fish. Although 14 days is the minimum, 21 days should be allowed as a safety measure if at all possible. Fish that have developed severe infestations from protozoan parasites such as ich should be quarantined for longer periods.

Important: Never add new fish to the quarantine tank once a quarantine has begun. Adding additional fish will only prolong the quarantine period because they will also need to be isolated for up to 21 days.

Water-Quality Testing and Monitoring
You will need to make regular water tests during the quarantine period to ensure optimum water quality. You should perform water tests including pH, ammonia, nitrite and nitrate. If the parameters are abnormal, such as high ammonia, make a partial water change and then retest the water. You can use ammonia removers such as zeolites in the filter if necessary. Use a good quality water conditioner during water changes to remove any chlorine or chloramine.

Treat water again with parasiticides and make partial water changes as required.

Tip: Water changes are an important part of the quarantine period. They serve to reduce built-up organics, dilute residues from chemicals used to treat the fish, and reduce the number of parasites in the tank.

Quarantine containers must be tightly covered with a screened top to prevent fish from jumping out of the tank.

Observing Your Fish
The fish must be examined several times each day to assess their progress. Fish treated for various diseases should begin showing improvement within three to five days.

Some fish's condition may improve faster than others in the group. However, even if one or two fish appear to have recovered, do not transfer them to the pond. More often than not, they are still carrying the disease agent. If you have any reason to believe the fish are still ill, hold them in quarantine for an additional seven to ten days. All fish must be quarantined for the full period without exception. If any of the fish should die, remove them promptly to prevent fouling of the water.

Feeding Your Fish During Quarantine
Be careful to feed your fish only lightly during the quarantine period. Often they will not eat for several days after transfer to the tank. However, you need not be alarmed at this; it is a natural response.

If you are treating your fish for a bacterial infection and using medicated food, it is important to feed exactly the amount required each day. It is also preferable to feed at approximately the same time. Medicated feeds are the best way to treat bacterial infections of koi. If you are treating with medicated foods, do not add additional antibiotics to the water to avoid possible drug toxicity. Check with your retailer on the availability of medicated foods for treating koi.

Transfer to the Pond

After the quarantine period has elapsed and any necessary treatments administered, the koi can be safely transferred to the pond. A minimum period of 14 to 21 days should elapse before this is done. You should reexamine the koi carefully prior to transferring them. If you have reason to believe that they are still parasitized or infected, conduct several more treatments and maintain them in quarantine for an additional seven to ten days.

Basic Treatments

Various chemicals are used to eradicate disease agents. Improperly used, these chemicals can be toxic to fish. Some have very narrow safety margins, so care must be exercised. Malachite green, for example, is an agent that must be used very cautiously.

While it is true that any chemical induces some stress in the fish under treatment, the problem is often minimal when the correct instructions are followed by the koi owner. It is desirable, whenever possible, to positively identify the disease agent before selecting a chemical treatment. Although this can seem complicated at first, some of the most common disease problems can be easily recognized (see page 80). Once the disease is identified, the appropriate medication can be selected for treatment.

Common table salt (noniodized only) is useful as a treatment for koi and is relatively safe. Its addition to water can perform two functions: easing osmoregulation and reducing stress. Salt added to water makes the ambient environment somewhat similar to the fish's body fluids, reducing the energy need. For this purpose, approximately 4 teaspoons per 10 gallons (20 grams per 36.4 L) of water will produce a 0.05 percent solution.

Salt can also be used to treat parasites, but must be applied at much stronger dosages. Special aquarium and pond salts are available from garden and pond centers and pet stores which give complete information on use for eradication of parasitic diseases.

Formalin/malachite green medications are commonly sold under various tradenames, including *RidIck*. These medications are excellent for the control of various protozoans that attack koi. The mixture is so effective that many parasites are eradicated with a single treatment.

Methylene blue is a standard chemical used for the eradication of parasites and fungus. It has been widely used for the control of external parasites, and is relatively nontoxic compared to formalin and malachite green. Its chief disadvantage is that it stains porous materials.

Organophosphates are excellent for use during quarantine to control external parasites, such as fish lice, copepods, and trematodes. The active ingredient is also present in various medications sold for eradication of internal parasites, such as anchorworms or flukes.

Various other medications are available for treating diseases. You should consult with your local pet retailer, garden and pond center, or koi breeder for additional information.

Using Chemicals Safely

There are some fundamental guidelines to using any type of chemical to treat koi. Not following these can interfere with the eradication of the disease, as well as posing possible toxicity hazards to the koi.

Any remedy must be used as directed on the label, and for the appropriate time period. Various environmental conditions, including pH, hardness, temperature, and other parameters should be considered, as they may have an effect on the efficacy of the chemical. For example, organophosphates are administered at lower dosages when added to water with an acid pH, as they remain active for longer periods under those conditions. In alkaline water, however, they are destroyed within 24 to 48 hours, so that under those conditions a greater amount must be administered more frequently.

A sequential treatment period should be followed using selected medications in order to remove any parasites present on koi. As will be discussed below, many parasitic diseases are quite common, and can become a serious problem if not eradicated promptly upon detection.

Disinfecting Equipment

One of the most important ways to prevent the transfer of diseases from quarantine tanks to your pond is to make sure anything that comes into contact with the quarantine aquarium is disinfected after use. Many disease agents affecting koi, including bacteria, protozoa, and viruses are easily transmitted. Just rinsing equipment in water is insufficient to destroy these agents. Nor is simple air drying of nets or buckets considered a method of disinfection. Many viruses and parasites, especially those that produce spores, can withstand air-drying. Disinfectants must be utilized to prevent disease transmission from one pond to another.

Tip: The plastic bags in which koi have been transported should never be reused.

Disinfectants

Various disinfectants are available commercially for treating nets and related pond equipment. The majority are either chlorine or surfactant-active compounds. The latter are popular, and include the benzalkonium chloride class of compounds. These disinfectants are safe, generally odorless, and nonstaining.

Surfactant-type disinfectants are widely used in hospitals, zoos, and food-production facilities. They have a wide spectrum of activity, and are effective against various disease-causing organisms. Concentrated solutions must be diluted prior to use. If the solution is used for net disinfection, it is important to rinse the net thoroughly with fresh water after disinfection and before use, as the disinfectant can be toxic. As with any chemical, the instructions provided on the label must be strictly followed to minimize any possible problems.

Chlorine-based products also give excellent results, and are routinely used for disinfecting equipment and nets. When added to water, these compounds are extremely effective in destroying common disease agents. Some disadvantages are their sharp odor and their propensity to corrode equipment, such as nets, with repeated usage. They are, however, readily available, inexpensive, and easily neutralized using common water dechlorinators containing sodium thiosulfate.

Common Koi Diseases and Treatments

Maintaining water quality is critical for good fish health. Deterioration of the aquatic environment leads to stress, decreased resistance, and the emergence of disease.

Stress and Its Effect on Fish Health

Research by fisheries scientists has shown that in natural populations there is a complex relationship between fish and the disease organisms that infect them. This accounts for the fact that fish in the wild can be found to harbor potential disease agents without exhibiting clinical signs of the disease. Thus it is often the case that newly purchased koi may appear to be in excellent health, but develop diseases after transport to your pond. Though they had previously been asymptomatic, the stress of the move depressed their immune responses, allowing the growth of the pathogenic organism.

Fish are well protected with both nonspecific and specific (immune system) defenses. As long as the fish is in good health, these protective mechanisms are fully capable of preventing development of the disease.

Stress is the overall physiological response of an organism to perceived danger. For example, when you net a fish or reach into its pond, you induce a stress response.

In response to stressors, an organism undergoes various complex internal chemical changes. These changes allow it to react quickly to situations of

immediate danger. If the stressful episodes are short and infrequent, the organism typically returns to normal quickly and shows no ill effects. But the stress response uses a lot of energy, and when such situations continue for too long, exhaustion can set in.

If the degree and duration of the stress is too great, damage, or even death, can occur. Stress has a profound effect on the health of the fish, with the immune system being especially vulnerable. Therefore, the stress response should be minimized whenever possible.

Diseases develop when there is an imbalance between the pathogen and the host, resulting from a decrease in immunity. This imbalance can be initiated by unfavorable conditions such as high concentrations of ammonia or carbon dioxide, low dissolved oxygen, excessive handling, crowding, and poor nutrition. Continual or chronic stress decreases the fish's resistance and predisposes them to disease. Certain conditions such as bacterial gill disease, abdominal distention, and *Chilodonella* infestations are mediated by stress. Their outbreak and development is correlated with unfavorable conditions such as poor water quality. Whenever you find a disease, test the water.

Identifying Diseases

Diseased fish will often demonstrate behavioral signs that can help in making a tentative diagnosis.

First, perform a series of standard water tests to ensure that the problem

Effective treatment for koi diseases requires careful identification of the signs associated with various diseases.

is not directly related to poor water quality. If it is, make necessary water changes. If the environmental parameters appear normal, you can then look into the possibility that the problem is being caused by parasites, bacteria, fungus, or viruses.

Many diseases are easy to diagnose by observing typical behavioral changes or body lesions. However, many of the lesions caused by parasites are similar in their appearance. Therefore recognition of the parasite is important in order to confirm the diagnosis.

Once the disease is identified, select an appropriate course of treatment. You may need to treat with an antimicrobial agent, or one designed to eradicate certain parasites. Some medications are *broad spectrum* and are effective against a wide range of pathogenic organisms. Others are only effective against one or a few.

Basic Medications and Techniques

Various medications are available commercially for the treatment of koi diseases. You should rely on your professional pet store owner, koi breeder, or professional pond and garden center for the proper selection and use of medications.

The majority of medications offered fall into two broad categories: antimicrobials (which include antibiotics) and parasiticides. Some proprietary medications can combine both types into one product. They may come in either powder, tablet, or liquid form.

Antimicrobials include a variety of drugs designed to control and eradicate microorganisms such as bacteria, fungi, and viruses. Their chemical activity is variable, but they generally interfere with the ability of the pathogenic organisms to make certain cellular components, such as their cell walls, by blocking protein synthesis. Several examples of antimicrobials

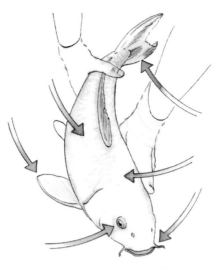

Carefully examine fish for signs of disease. Look for any lesions on the tail, parasites on the body surface, ragged fins, tumors on the head, cloudy eyes, or abrasions on the snout.

used for the treatment of fish diseases include tetracycline, oxalinic acid, sarafloxacin, and kanamycin.

Parasiticides are medications indicated for the treatment of parasitic disease agents such as protozoans

This koi was transferred to a shallow plastic tub to facilitate inspection of several lesions on the body surface.

(*Chilodonella, Ichthyobodo*, etc.), trematodes (flukes), tapeworms, leeches, and copepods. Various commercially produced parasiticides are available for treating fish in ponds and quarantine tanks. Some commonly used parasiticides are salt, malachite green, formalin, metronidazole, and acriflavine.

Combined formulations: Some brands of fish medications combine both parasiticides and antimicrobials into proprietary formulations. In developing these combinations, manufacturers mix various compatible medications to control a wide spectrum of disease agents, from protozoans to flukes and copepods. The use of these medications eliminates the need for individual treatment of the disease with separately administered medications. For example, a multicomponent medication could include malachite green for controlling protozoans, an antimicrobial such as tetracycline for treating bacterial infections, and an organophosphate for controlling anchorworm.

Administration Techniques

Disease outbreaks can be treated using various methods, including addition to the water, administration in the food, or injection. The latter technique is excellent for treating fish, but requires training and should be used with caution.

The most common method is addition of the medication to the water. This mode of administration is subdivided into dips and extended baths.

Dipping is characterized by an exposure period ranging from several seconds to several minutes. The fish is removed from the pond, placed in a basin of water to which the medication has been added, then removed after the predetermined treatment period. The dip method is repeated several times, depending on the disease and the type of drug. The disadvantage of

this method is that it is stressful, since the fish must be handled as well as exposed to higher drug concentrations. This method is therefore not as safe as other means, and should be used with caution. When using dips, it is essential to observe the fish's behavior throughout the treatment period. Always terminate the treatment promptly if the fish become severely stressed.

Extended baths are a safer and more commonly used method. The fish are exposed to a more dilute solution of the medication for a longer period, generally lasting several hours or more depending on the type of drug, its toxicity, and the disease being treated.

Adding medications to the food is a useful method of administration, often used to eradicate systemic bacterial infections and internal parasites. To eradicate tapeworms, for example, a drug must be administered in the food. Several commercial food preparations are sold that incorporate antibacterials or parasiticides.

Treatment Guidelines

The following guidelines should be followed whenever treating koi in ponds or in quarantine facilities. It is important to understand that treating fish is a serious matter, and must be approached with caution. Carelessness could result in possible mortalities.

Various problems can arise during treatment, including inhibition of the activity of the nitrifying bacteria, water-quality deterioration, and possible sensitivity of the fish to the treatment agent.

Identify the Disease
Prior to Treatment

Although as a koi pond owner you are not likely to become an expert in disease diagnosis, you should be able to recognize several of the most common koi disease problems. Identifying the disease prior to treatment allows the selection of a more appropriate treatment regime. While a shotgun approach to disease treatments will sometimes work, it will more often be unsuccessful, and subject the fish to the stress of an unnecessary drug.

Avoid Adding Chemicals to Ponds

It is preferable to treat diseased fish in separate quarantine facilities. The addition of chemicals to ponds should be avoided, although this is not always possible. Chemicals added to the pond can cause various problems, including damage to plants and biological filters, and necessitate the need for large-volume water changes between treatments.

Prior to using any chemical in the pond or quarantine tank, you should be aware of possible effects on the filter bacteria. Some chemicals will cause a suppression or complete cessation of the filter-bed activity, with the subsequent increase in the level of toxic ammonia. Two drugs known to adversely affect the biological filter bacteria are methylene blue and erythromycin. You should follow instructions carefully on the use of these and other drugs that you purchase for pond use.

Observe the Behavior of the Fish During Treatment

Although it is intended to cure a disease, the addition of any chemical to water is nonetheless stressful to fish. The toxicity of drugs varies according to the type and strength of the medication. It is important to be cautious whenever using a chemical for the first time in a pond or treatment facility. A general rule is to test medications with a small group of fish prior to administration to a larger group. It is best to perform the treatment earlier in the day, so that you can observe their behavior. If they appear unduly

stressed, make an immediate water change. It is recommended that you consult your retailer on the proper use and precautions associated with chemicals intended for use in ponds.

Continue Water Testing During Treatment

Routine tests such as pH, ammonia, dissolved oxygen, etc., should be made throughout the duration of the treatment. A decline of water quality only worsens existing infections by further lowering the koi's resistance. Such conditions work against a rapid recovery of the fish under treatment.

Make Water Changes

In addition to water tests, a regular series of water changes should be made throughout the treatment. Generally, a partial water change is required every 24 to 36 hours, after which the medicine is again administered. Information on the frequency of water changes is usually detailed on the medication package.

There are various reasons why water changes are necessary during treatment of koi. Most importantly, water changes dilute concentrations of various toxic chemicals, including ammonia, organics, and degradation products resulting from the decomposition of the chemicals used during treatment. Reducing organics is especially important, since they bind up many chemicals such as malachite green, rendering the chemical useless for parasite control. Water changes also dilute the concentration of parasites or bacteria, helping to accelerate recovery of the koi.

Discontinue Chemical Filtration During Treatments

Activated carbon is effective in removing various chemicals from the water, including such medications as malachite green, formalin, and antibi-

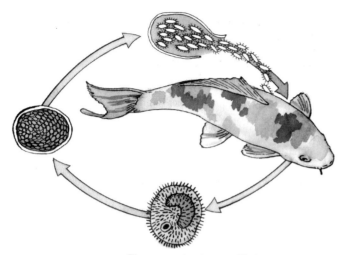

The proper treatment of koi diseases requires an understanding of the life cycle of various troublesome parasites. The common protozoan, Ichthyophthirius multifiliis develops as small white spots on the koi's body. Upon maturation, the parasite drops off the fish to the pond bottom where it encysts and releases small tomites that can reinfect the koi.

otics. It is essential to discontinue use of any activated carbon in your mechanical filters during fish treatments. However, the filters themselves should remain in full operation. Upon completion of the treatment, and after a water change, new chemically active media can be restored to the filter.

Infectious Diseases

Though many diseases affect koi, not all are serious and life-threatening. They are divided into two groups: infectious diseases, those easily transmitted to other fish, and noninfectious diseases such as tumors and nutritional deficiencies.

Infectious diseases are caused by a number of different types of organisms, among which the most important are parasites, including protozoans; various kinds of worms; and crustaceans; bacteria; fungi; and viruses.

Protozoa

The protozoans are the most common disease agents affecting koi. These are one-celled, microscopic organisms that can reproduce rapidly in ponds. Protozoa are classified primarily by their morphological characteristics. Perhaps the most important characteristic for our purposes is the presence or absence of *cilia*. These are tiny, hairlike projections from the surface of the body, used primarily for locomotion. Many parasitic protozoa are ciliated. A smaller number have longer, whiplike *flagella*, with which they move around. While most of these creatures are free-swimming and solitary, some will group themselves together in *colonies*.

Some parasites cannot survive outside of the host. These are called *obligate* parasites. If they can survive without their preferred hosts they are referred to as *opportunistic*.

Though any pond will be filled with protozoa, most will not be pathogenic. Once a dangerous variety has been introduced, its development is highly dependent on the water temperature. Hence, the protozoa's life cycle can take as little as several days in high-temperature water, or weeks, even months, at colder water temperatures.

Some diseases caused by protozoa are:

White spot disease, which is caused by a ciliated organism called *Ichthyophthirius multifiliis*, nicknamed "ich" (pronounced "ik"). It attacks the skin and gills. The disease is serious, and must be treated rapidly to prevent mortalities.

Infected fish are listless, have clamped fins, (i.e., the fins have collapsed onto the body), lose their normal color, and are covered with small white spots on their body and fins. These can be most readily detected on the darker portions of the fish's body. Affected koi often congregate near

84

areas of water turbulence. They can also be observed to scratch themselves frequently on objects in the pond.

The life cycle of the parasite includes both attached and free-swimming forms. The control of ich focuses on the eradication of the free-swimming form.

The attached parasites, which can attain a size of 1 mm, drop off the fish when mature and sink to the bottom of the pond, where they encyst. Division occurs within the cyst, and a number of free-swimming individuals develop. The cyst eventually ruptures, releasing the parasites into the water, where they seek a fish to infect. The time required to complete the life cycle is temperature-dependent: The higher the temperature, the faster the cycle. For example, in water of 70° to 79°F (21°–26°C), the life cycle is completed in less than a week, while in water at 50°F (10°C), the life cycle is extended to over a week.

Various commercial medications are effective for controlling ich. The active ingredients in these formulations are most often formalin, malachite green, salt, and potassium permanganate.

Preparations such as *Ridlck*, containing formalin and malachite green in combination, are excellent for controlling this pathogen.

Trichodinids: *Trichodina* and related species such as *Trichodonella* are troublesome ciliated protozoa that commonly parasitize koi. They are capable of causing damage to the skin and gills, leading to secondary bacterial infections. They have been implicated as the precursor to the development of *ulcer disease.*

Affected fish frequently scratch themselves on the sides or bottom of the pond, have clamped fins, lose their normal coloration, and have difficult respiration. The skin develops small reddened ulcerations that gradually enlarge.

Most of the medications used for the treatment of ich are also suitable for eradication of trichodina. The parasites are sensitive to malachite green or formalin.

Because trichodinids multiply by simple cell division with no free-swimming form, usually only one or two treatments are required.

Chilodonella *(Chilodeonella cyprini)* is a ciliated protozoan commonly affecting koi and goldfish. It is an obligate parasite that inhabits the skin and gills. When examined microscopically, it appears heart-shaped or oval. Infected fish develop a noticeable bluish-white opaqueness of the skin, with excess mucus secretion. They will tend to scrape themselves on the pond bottom. Increased lethargy and an increased respiratory rate is often observed. Mortality is rapid, especially among juvenile fish. Treatments using malachite green, formalin, or salt dips are required for eradication of the parasite.

Epistylis is a ciliate that is known to attach to koi. The protozoan is not considered an obligate parasite, but will multiply under certain conditions, forming large, stalked colonies.

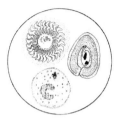

Common protozoan parasites of koi: *(clockwise from the top left)* Trichodina, Chilodonella *and* Ichthyophthirius.

Chilodonella *primarily affects the gills, causing extensive tissue damage and predisposing the fish to secondary bacterial infection.*

Attachment to the host invites secondary infection by bacteria.

Koi affected by *Epistylis* develop white tuft-like areas, resembling fungus. As they grow, the areas become ulcerated, with a reddish ring surrounding the white area.

The presence of *Epistylis* is almost always associated with poor water quality and high water temperatures. High levels of organic material in the pond water favor its development. It is easily controlled by the use of formalin-based medications.

Ichthyobodo necatrix, formerly known as *Costia*, is a small, flagellated protozoan. It is a troublesome parasite, attacking fish that have been previously stressed. The Japanese refer to this disease as *dorokaburi*, or "slime disease."

Affected fish develop a whitish film on their skin, are listless, and hold their fins close to their body. Conspicuous red lesions can also be present, and the fish will repeatedly scratch themselves on the pond bottom. Rapid, labored respiration is not uncommon.

Like other protozoa, *Ichthyobodo* is sensitive to medications containing malachite green, salt, or formalin.

Sporozoans are a group of troublesome parasites whose life cycle involves the production of large numbers of tough spores that can survive for long periods without a host. Although they are not as commonly encountered as other protozoa, it is important to be able to recognize the signs of infection. They form white nodules on the fins, skin, and gills, and produce light-colored lesions in the muscles.

Affected fish usually show very little alteration in their normal behavior. An increased respiratory rate can be observed when the parasites invade the gills.

No safe and effective treatments are available for sporozoan infestations. Affected fish must be removed from the pond to prevent possible transmission of the disease.

Coccidians are another group of protozoa capable of causing severe losses. The most frequently seen coccidial disease is known as nodular coccidiosis, caused by the organism *Eimeria cyprini*. Young koi are the most likely victims, sustaining damage to the intestinal lining.

Affected fish can show a loss of color, have sunken eyes, and become thin. A yellowish color in the feces is characteristic of the disease. Various medications have been tried, but the disease is still considered untreatable. Affected fish must be be removed from the pond to prevent transmission to other koi.

Platyhelminths

The platyhelminths include various parasitic worms such as flukes and tapeworms. Many have complex life cycles requiring more than one host.

Trematodes, or flukes, are a class of parasites divided according to their life cycle into two major groups: the *monogenes* and the *digenes*. Monogenetic trematodes are external parasites of the skin and gills which require only one host to complete their life cycle. The digenetic group is made up of internal parasites. They have a complex life cycle requiring more than one host.

Monogenetic trematodes: The pond owner should be primarily concerned with the monogenetic flukes, as they are common parasites of koi and other fish and can cause serious mortality increases.

Gyrodactylus and *Dactylogyrus* are two monogenetic genera that commonly infest koi. Virtually every imported fish carries these parasites. Koi bred in the United States can also carry the organisms, with infestations becoming especially serious during the summer months.

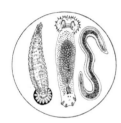

Common parasitic worms: (left to right) leech, monogenetic fluke, nematode.

The flukes attach to fish by means of a special attachment organ, called a *haptor*, that is equipped with hooks.

Affected fish show variable behavioral changes, depending on the severity of the infection. The most common clinical signs are increased rate of respiration, dull coloration, and excessive scratching on the pond bottom or on various objects. Serious infections involving the gills result in hemorrhaging, skin damage, and secondary bacterial infection.

Monogenetic trematodes are easily eradicated with commercial medications containing formalin. Products containing organophosphates, mebendazole, or praoziquantel are also useful for control of monogenetic flukes. You should consult a pond-fish specialist or your local retailer for information regarding medications for the control of these parasites.

Digenetic trematodes have a complex life cycle, with a number of larval forms and several hosts. The first form, known as a *miracidium*, parasitizes snails. Here it develops into a cercariae. This form parasitizes a second host, either forming a *metacercariae* or maturing directly into the adult parasite. *Metacecariae* appear as nodules on various parts of the body, including eyes, gills, muscles, and skin. Eventually they transform into adults, which migrate to the intestinal tract.

Affected fish become listless, and a pattern of slow mortalities can develop. If the parasite is present in the gills, these will be pale, with swellings or cysts. Nodules can be present on the skin as well as on internal organs.

Generally, digenetic trematodes are not considered to be serious parasites of koi. Keeping snails out of the koi pond is a simple but effective way to prevent the development of the disease. Once the parasites have infested the fish, the disease is basically untreatable.

Cestodes, or tapeworms, are flattened worms whose body is composed of a head and a number of segments called *proglottids*. The head bears an organ called a *scolex*, with which the worm attaches to the inner wall of the intestine. Tapeworms have complex life cycles requiring several hosts. Koi can be the intermediate or final host, depending on the species of tapeworm. The final hosts of some species are either birds or mammals. Larval forms can encyst in the peritoneal cavity or other areas of the fish's body. The most common cestode species parasitizing koi are *Bothriocephalus* and *Caryophyllaeus*.

Infestations are difficult to diagnose. Very few behavioral signs are observed. Severely infested fish can appear emaciated, though they appear to eat normally. The presence of tapeworms is usually confirmed only by necropsy.

Most of the medications recommended for treatment must be added to the food in order to kill these internal parasites effectively. Recent research using the drug called Praziquantel has indicated that it rapidly eradicates tapeworms from the gut. The drug is simply added to the water for use in a bath treatment.

Nematodes

The nematodes are slender, unsegmented roundworms. In the larval form nematodes can be found in practically any organ or tissue of a fish. They are most common in the musculature, intestine, and liver.

Their life cycle involves intermediate hosts, the first usually being a copepod or insect. If a koi eats the intermediate hosts containing the larval nematodes, the worms will take up residence in the fish's gut. If the worms use the fish as an intermediate host, they will be found coiled in small nodules in the tissues or organs.

Affected fish exhibit poor appetite and loss of color. There are few drugs which are totally effective in eradicating nematodes. The best treatment is addition of the drug Panacur at a concentration of 0.25 percent.

Annelids

The annelids are a group of worms containing both free-living and parasitic species. The best known of the free-living annelids is the common earthworm. The only type that is troublesome to koi are the leeches.

Leeches are external parasites with a segmented body and anterior and posterior suckers. The posterior sucker is larger, while the smaller anterior sucker contains the oral apparatus, with specialized organs and a mouth. Most of the species affecting koi are visible with the naked eye.

Two common crustacean parasites: Argulus, the fish louse (top), and Lernaea cyprinacea, *the common anchorworm.*

The parasites feed on the host's blood, and when present in large enough numbers, especially in young fish, they can cause anemia. Leeches are more of an annoyance than a serious problem. They are, however, known to transmit bacterial diseases through the wounds they cut in the fish's skin.

Leeches can be eradicated by using a variety of drugs sold on the market.

Tip: Always quarantine plants before placing them in the pond to prevent introduction of leeches or leech eggs.

Crustaceans

Crustaceans are arthropods. Among the family are such well-known animals as shrimps and lobsters, but they also include numerous parasitic species. They are capable of causing severe tissue damage.

Argulus, or fish lice, have flat bodies and can crawl freely over the fish's skin. In appearance they resemble flattened scales. Eggs are laid on sub-

merged vegetation and other objects in the pond.

Affected fish show damaged, reddened skin surfaces and pinpoint hemorrhages. Koi must be carefully examined for the presence of small, mottled, leaflike moving scales on their skin. Fish lice can also invade the gills, so increased and labored respiration are signs associated with infestation. Many species are large enough to see with the naked eye or with the aid of a low-power magnifier.

Treatment is with a variety of commercial medications containing one or more of the following active ingredients: formalin, organophosphates, or potassium permanganate.

Copepods are small crustaceans, many of which are parasitic on koi. Specialized holdfast organs are present and the mouth parts are adapted to piercing the fish's body.

The anchorworm, *Lernaea cyprinacea*, is a common copepod parasite of koi. Although referred to as anchorworms, they are not really worms. Mature females produce eggs in strings, and these, trailing from the body of the fish, are diagnostic. Newly hatched larvae are immediately capable of infecting fish.

The presence of a few parasites is not serious, but untreated fish are likely to develop secondary bacterial infections.

These parasites can be controlled using various commercial medications containing formalin and organophosphates. The goal of treatment is the eradication of the free-swimming juvenile form. When only a few adult worms are present on the fish, they can be carefully removed using forceps.

Bacteria

Bacteria are unicellular, microscopic organisms commonly found in soil and water. They vary in shape and reproduce by simple division. For purposes of identification they are divided into

88

three groups, based on their staining characteristics when slides are prepared for viewing under a microscope. The groups are: gram-positive, gram-negative, and acid-fast. The majority of bacterial diseases in fish are caused by gram-negative bacteria.

Bacterial infections are largely initiated by deteriorating water conditions, inducing stress which lowers normal resistance. Damaged skin is a common site for the establishment of bacteria. If left untreated, the infection progresses internally and can become systemic.

Only the more common bacterial diseases affecting koi are discussed in this section.

Ulcer disease, also known as dropsy or abdominal distention, is usually caused by *Aeromonas* or *Pseudomonas* bacteria. Affected fish show ulceration of the body, a swollen abdomen, protruding scales, and swollen eyes. The bases of the fins can become inflamed. Fish tend to be listless, stop eating, and lose their normal coloration.

Disease outbreaks are correlated with environmental factors. In koi, outbreaks usually occur in the spring, but the disease can also occur during the summer, especially if the fish are stressed by chronically low oxygen concentrations.

Infected fish should be treated by adding appropriate antibiotics to the food. The addition of antibiotics to the pond water is not recommended since the disease is an internal process, and most medications are unable to be absorbed from water in sufficient quantity to be effective. Tetracyline or oxytetracycline should be added to the food. Medicated foods are commercially available.

Bacterial gill disease can be caused by a number of species, the most common being *myxobacteria*. The condition has been linked to overcrowding, high levels of organics,

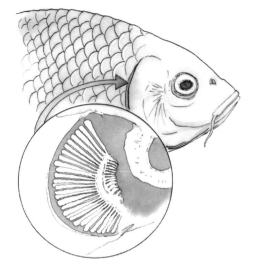

Gill disease can be caused by numerous types of bacteria. Infection results in the destruction and erosion of the delicate filaments. Deteriorating water quality has been linked to the development of this disease.

and other related environmental conditions, and can cause extensive mortalities. Some studies have shown that in the earlier stages of development, progression can be reversed simply by reducing the population and

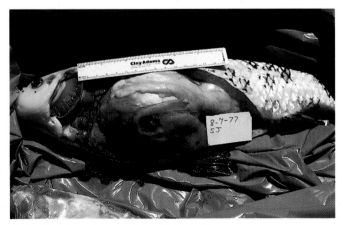

Swim bladder enlargement is often associated with bacterial and viral infections.

89

flushing the pond with new water. The problem is uncommon in ponds that have low fish populations and good water quality. Outbreaks have also been correlated with abnormally high temperatures.

Affected fish appear lethargic and become abnormally pale, with excess mucus present on the skin. Respiratory distress is common, and infected individuals can be observed near the pond surface or in agitated areas. Large white areas of dead tissue are found in the gills. Secondary fungal infections are also observed. Large quantities of bacteria are seen in microscopic examination of skin scrapings.

Several approaches can be used in controlling bacterial gill disease. Antibacterials have been found useful, including nitrofurans such as nitrofura-

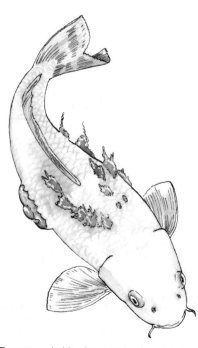

Fungus on koi is characterized by the presence of cotton-like growths that develop on injured areas of the body.

zone. The best approach is preventive: keeping the fish population low and well fed, and maintaining a properly operational filter.

Mycobacteriosis is a well-known disease, having been reported in koi as early as 1897. It is caused by the organism *Mycobacteria*, which produces characteristic lesions, called granulomas, in the internal organs. The condition is difficult to diagnose, as the signs are not always specific. Mycobacteriosis is a chronic and progressive disease. Fish develop ulcerations, swollen eyes, and abdominal distention. Diagnosis is only confirmed from an internal examination of the fish, which is itself a lethal procedure.

There is no therapy for mycobacteriosis. Fish suspected of having the disease should be removed from the pond to prevent transmission to other fish.

Fungal Infections

Fungal infections are frequently encountered in koi, usually appearing after transport or in association with other diseases, especially those involving parasites. Fungi are generally secondary invaders, typically developing on wounds. Though they get their start on the skin, they can progress internally and cause extensive damage.

There are many species of fungi, but the two most important types are *Saprolegnia* and *Branchiomyces*.

Saprolegniasis is a fairly common condition, characterized by the presence of whitish threads on the skin and fins of koi. It can be quite prevalent during the spawning season. The fungus is recognized by its cottony-white appearance, and is easily seen with the naked eye. The large, grayish-white lesions sometimes have a reddish perimeter. Algae can sometimes be seen associated with the lesions. This fungus is usually found on the skin, but also occurs on damaged gill tissue. Infection of the gills is extremely serious and must be treated immediately to prevent mortality.

During early stages of the disease, the fungus can be eradicated quickly, but it is more difficult to cure as it progressively invades the fish's body. Commercial medications containing malachite green are particularly effective, and methylene blue, salt, and formalin are also useful.

Branchiomycosis, called *erakusaribyo* by the Japanese, is a disease of the gills. Unlike *Saprolegnia*, this fungus is partial to intravascular tissue, and invades the gills directly. It is believed that infection is initiated by ingestion of fungal spores.

Affected fish show extreme respiratory distress and hemorrhages, and patches of dead gill tissue are seen. Fish can succumb to the disease within several days.

Currently there is no known treatment. It is important to isolate any suspected fish.

Viral Infections

Viruses are extremely small infective agents that can only multiply within the living cells of the host. The best known fish viruses infect salmon and trout, but several are known to attack koi.

Viral infections are best avoided by carefully quarantining fish suspected of carrying them. It is impossible to diagnose the majority of viral infections from physical examination, although a few produce characteristic lesions.

Spring viremia of carp (SVCV) has often been described as dropsy or abdominal distention. The disease was once thought to be a complex condition, initiated by bacteria and followed by a viral invasion, but it is now known to be caused by a single agent, *Rhabdovirus carpio*.

Various signs are associated with the disease, among which are swollen eyes, hemorrhages of the skin and gills, inability to swim, and swollen abdomen. Affected fish also become darker in color and stay in areas of the pond where the water is agitated. Koi of any age group can be affected, but the disease is particularly serious in younger koi. The disease tends to be most prevalent in the early spring as water temperatures begin to increase. Extensive mortalities are common.

The disease is highly contagious. Viral particles are shed into the water via the feces, generally entering the fish through the gills. Fish that survive the infection can be carriers for life. Neither treatment nor control is known. However, treatment with appropriate antibiotics can help to resolve any secondary bacterial infections. Suspected fish must be removed from the pond.

Tip: The disease can easily be misdiagnosed as intestinal blockage caused by overfeeding.

Carp pox has been known for over 400 years, yet it is not often recognized as a viral disease by koi pond owners. It is caused by a virus belonging to the *herpes* group, is considered chronic and not life-threatening, and often develops during the early spring season.

Affected fish develop small, white, opaque, plaque-like raised areas on various parts of the body. These gradually enlarge. The lesions are smooth, and can be tinged pink due to a heavy development of capillaries within the tissue.

There is no treatment, but the lesions often disappear as water temperatures increase.

Lymphocystis, like SVCV, is a well-known viral disease of fish. The characteristic hard, mulberry-like nodules on the body and fins make this the easiest viral disease to diagnose with the naked eye. It is a chronic condition, and is rarely fatal. No treatment is known. The virus spreads when the

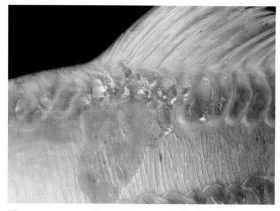

Carp pox, caused by a virus, results in the development of plaque-like lesions on the body.

Tumors are classified as either benign or malignant. The benign tumor on this koi can be removed surgically.

nodules rupture, releasing viral particles into the water.

Noninfectious Diseases

A number of disease syndromes are classified as noninfectious, arising generally from changes in the environment, poor handling, inadequate nutrition, and genetic and congenital anomalies. Various types of tumors can also occur in koi, most of which are not caused by infectious organisms.

Tumors

Tumors are aberrant growths of cells that develop in an uncoordinated and uncontrolled manner. They can appear on the body surface or in any organ, and arise from different types of cells.

Tumors are classified as benign or malignant. Benign tumors are noninvasive, and remain encapsulated at the site of origin. Malignant tumors spread rapidly, destroying normal body tissue. Such tumors can arise at one point of the body and quickly disperse to other areas.

There are many causes of tumors. Some are related to infection by biological disease agents. Other possible causes include genetic predisposition, exposure to carcinogenic chemicals, diet, and modifications in the environment. The origin of many types of tumors is unknown.

Only two of the tumor types that most commonly affect koi will be discussed in this section: pigmented skin-cell tumors and liver tumors.

Pigmented skin-cell tumors are characterized by the appearance of multiple tumors on the dorsal portion of the body. The condition has been referred to by Japanese writers as "Hi-eating worm," although this is a misnomer, since it has nothing to do with worms.

The cause of the disease is unknown and the condition is untreatable. It is malignant, and rapidly spreads to other body surfaces. The most common tumor of this group is the melanoma, which arises from cells containing the dark pigment melanin. These tumors are soft, black, pigmented, and raised on the body surface.

Liver tumors arise from various cells in the liver, and are commonly found in koi. Several researchers have suggested that the tumors could arise from food contaminated with aflatoxin,

Most commonly, darkly pigmented swellings on the dorsal region of koi are diagnosed as melanomas, a malignant type of tumor.

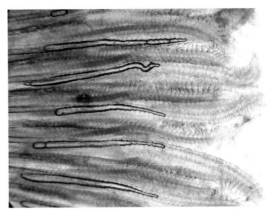

Gas bubble disease is caused by supersaturation of gas in pond water. Note the silvery colored areas (emboli) in the gill filaments.

which is produced by certain fungi. Affected fish often show a distended abdomen. The condition is untreatable.

Gas-Bubble Disease

This condition is associated with the supersaturation of gases in water, usually nitrogen. The Japanese refer to it as *kihobyo*. The disease syndrome in koi ponds is caused by leaks in valves, pumps, and airlines. It can also be caused by sudden temperature changes or heavy algal blooms in the summer.

Affected fish develop bubbles of gas in the skin, eyes, gills, and internal organs, including the swim bladder. A common sign is the presence of gas emboli in the capillaries of the gills. These emboli can be seen without the aid of a microscope.

Nutritional Diseases

Koi are subject to a wide variety of nutritional diseases if their diets are improperly formulated. The most serious cases commonly occur in young fish. Nutritional diseases tend to develop slowly over months or years.

Nutritional diseases can be prevented by providing well-rounded diets, a variety of foods and avoiding poorly formulated foods.

Toxic Conditions

Various types of toxic conditions traced to water quality have been discussed previously. For example, high concentrations of ammonia and nitrite can adversely affect fish. Hydrogen-sulfide toxicity is a serious problem associated with poor cleaning procedures and incorrect filter-bed maintenance.

Insecticides and herbicides are toxic to koi and can be introduced to the pond by adjacent spraying of shrubs and trees.

Tip: Advise your neighbors to alert you if they are planning to use insecticides, as airborne chemicals can be blown into the pond by the wind.

Breeding Koi

At some point most koi hobbyists become interested in breeding their fish. By providing suitable water quality and nutrition, and following the procedures outlined in this chapter, you will find this to be an enjoyable task. The investment of a modest amount of time should enable you to produce, over several generations, some excellent-quality koi with beautiful colors and patterns.

While a complete discussion of breeding techniques and genetics is beyond the scope of this book, several examples will be given to illustrate how certain traits are inherited in koi. Let us start with an overview of sexing and breeding.

Although a variety of spawning methods are utilized, most breeders will partition off areas of the pond and place the breeding-age fish in an isolated section with *spawning medium*. The eggs are left in the pond to hatch. When the fry reach a certain size, they are moved to a separate pond.

The developing fish are carefully observed by the breeder with an eye toward selecting the best colors, patterns, and especially for new characteristics.

Sexing

Koi reach sexual maturity within three years. They mate from spring and early summer through the fall, the breeding season being longer or shorter depending on the local climate.

Though it is difficult to determine the sex of juveniles, the signs in mature fish are fairly easy to spot. Male koi tend to have more slender bodies than females, and have protruding pectoral fins, with the pectoral rays somewhat pointed. During the breeding season they also develop numerous protrusions, resembling spots, on the pectoral fins. Do not confuse these spots with the various diseases discussed above. These protrusions are *only* found on the fins.

Females have a more robust, rounded body form, and pectoral fins which are somewhat rounded as well. During the breeding season they will become even more robust in appearance as their eggs develop.

Breeding Methods

You can breed your fish in the main pond or in a special breeding tank. Many hobbyists prefer the latter method. In either case, the first step is to select the best-colored koi and isolate them in a small area with a depth of approximately 24 inches (61 cm) or slightly less. The breeding tank needs to be of sufficient size, at least 6 to 8 feet (1.8–2.4 m) long and 4 to 6 feet (1.2–1.8 m) wide, to permit a reasonable water depth.

A tank this size will easily accommodate a breeding pair. Much larger tanks are required if you are going to breed a number of fish at the same time.

Tip: The tank should be equipped with a cover, preferably of heavy netting affixed to a sturdy wood frame. This is needed both to protect the fish from predators and to avoid the possibility of the fish jumping out of the container. Never cover a container with a solid cover, such as hard plastic, as the koi could become injured if they jump.

The Spawning Medium

A spawning medium should be added to the breeding enclosure. Aquatic plants with long roots, such as water hyacinths, are excellent, as are numerous other plants. Artificial media are available as well. Redwood branches have also been used as spawning media in California. Several branches are tied together, then placed in the pond in the evening. The koi will scatter their eggs among the spawning media. Once the eggs are attached, the branches can easily be removed and placed in a tank for hatching. However, these branches should not be left in the pond too long as they can release organics into the water.

The Spawning Pair

Place the fish in the spawning pond or breeding tank. Courtship will become evident within several days or even several hours. This activity can

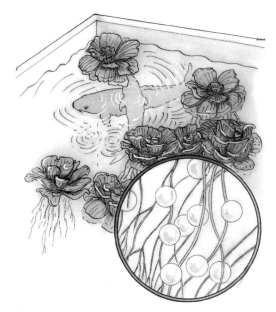

The sticky eggs are deposited on the spawning media placed in the pond or spawning tank.

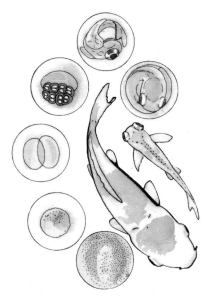

The stages of koi egg development (clockwise from bottom).

become quite pronounced, as the males chase the females around the pond. As the tempo of courtship increases, it signals that deposition of the eggs will occur within a short period of time.

Eggs tend to be laid in the early morning hours, coincident with lower water temperatures. Koi will scatter their eggs anywhere in the pond, but prefer plants and artificial spawning materials. The eggs are very sticky and readily attach to anything. Koi are very prolific spawners and a female can deposit over 100,000 eggs. Many of these, however, will not survive. Some will be infertile and others will be attacked by parasites, fungi, bacteria, or consumed by predators, and many of the hatchling fry will never reach the juvenile stage.

It is important that the the eggs be separated from the breeders after spawning, as the parents like to eat

Newly deposited koi eggs affixed to redwood branches.

The culling process involves selecting fish with the best colors and patterns.

them. The eggs should be maintained in clean, aerated water with a constant water temperature. Alternatively, the adults can be removed and returned to the main pond.

Hatching of the Eggs

Hatching usually occurs within a week at temperatures of 65° to 75°F (18.3°–23.9°C). Too low a temperature will prevent the normal development of the eggs. You should not expect all the eggs to hatch. Infertile eggs will turn a milky white color.

Fungi readily attack fish eggs, so it is recommended that an antifungal chemical be added to their container. Several dyes are useful for controlling fungi, including malachite green, acriflavine, and methylene blue. These products are available commercially under various tradenames at pet stores, koi farms, and garden centers. Care must be exercised in their use, however, due to their toxicity.

For the first several days after hatching the fry will obtain their food from the yolk sac. After this they will start feeding on small organisms in the water. They can also be fed supplementary high-protein food powders, algae, or newly hatched brine shrimp. They must be fed frequently throughout the day.

Good water quality must be maintained. Special care must be taken if the fry are being raised in a tank, as these smaller containers will foul more rapidly than a full-sized pond. Uneaten food must be removed frequently from the tank bottom. Ensure that the water is properly filtered and well aerated. The standard water tests, such as pH and ammonia, should be frequently performed.

Tip: Intake siphons from filters must have a fine netting placed over their ends to prevent the fry from being sucked into the filter.

96

Culling

The fry will grow rapidly. You could easily have many thousands of fish surviving from the spawn. This is obviously too many, and you will need to cull extensively. If you are after the best koi, you could end up keeping less than 25 percent of the hatchlings. The Japanese typically cull even more rigorously, keeping less than 10 percent of the original spawn.

The problem with rigorous culling is what to do with the excess fish. Bear in mind that in nature very few fish survive. The reproductive strategy of the carp is to produce hundreds of thousands of eggs—precisely because only the strongest and best-adapted have any chance of reaching maturity. By the same token, you should not attempt to keep every fish. Pet stores are always interested in obtaining "feeder fish" to sell as live food to aquarium hobbyists. Excess fish can also be donated to other koi pond owners.

The culling process involves selecting only fish with the best color and patterns. The Japanese divide the process into several steps, with the first culling selecting for overall color. Later, another culling selects for the best patterns. This is repeated as often as required to leave only the best specimens.

Before selecting for color, deformed or weak fish should be removed. They should also be sorted according to size. This is important, since koi have a tendency to be cannibalistic.

After approximately three months the juvenile fish should be culled for color. If some of the fish in the spawn are of the *doitsu* type, the culling process should include selection for the best scale patterns.

Important: Never release excess fish into local ponds or streams. This could disrupt the ecological balance of native flora and fauna.

Color and Pattern Inheritance

The Japanese have excelled in producing the majority of the available high-quality koi. Year after year new varieties and types are produced by koi enthusiasts. They are the result of intensive breeding programs, involving the careful selection of breeding stock over many generations.

Inheritance can be quite complicated. However, information on how some characteristics are inherited in koi is becoming more readily available to amateur koi pond owners, though much of this data has not been scientifically documented. Commercial breeders have closely guarded the details on the inheritance of their proprietary colors and patterns.

Basic Genetics

As with all other organisms, the traits passed on to the progeny are encoded in genes arranged on chromosomes located in the nuclei of cells. The chromosomes are paired, the number of paired chromosomes being unique to the species. From each pair of chromosomes, one from the male and one from the female is passed on to the progeny. Thus, when an egg is fertilized by a sperm, the full number of chromosomes is restored. The expression of traits such as sex, scalation, color, and pattern is referred to as the *phenotype*—the appearance of the trait in the animal. The *genotype*, however, refers to the actual composition of the chromosomes in the animal.

Sex Determination

The difference between genotype and phenotype is best explained by an example of how sex is determined. Both sexes have a pair of chromosomes that code for sex. In males the pair is made up of dissimilar chromosomes, named X and Y. Females, on the other hand, have two X chromosomes. As the female has only X chromosomes to contribute, the sex of the progeny is dependent on which sex chromosome is donated by the male. If the male contributes a Y chromosome the offspring will be a male (XY). But if the male contributes an X it will be female (XX). Because the sperm carry an equal number of X and Y chromosomes, it is equally likely that the sex of the offspring will be male or female. (Geneticists express this as a 50/50 probability.)

From this basic example we can move on to a more complex illustration: the inheritance of scalation in koi.

Scalation Inheritance

Previously it was mentioned that some koi, called leather koi, lack scales. Geneticists use the convention of uppercase and lowercase letters when discussing the genotype of an animal. The uppercase letter means the gene is *dominant*; the lowercase letter denotes a *recessive* gene. If the pair of genes for any given trait are mixed (one dominant and one recessive), the phenotype will reveal the dominant characteristic. Only when both genes are recessive can the recessive characteristic appear.

In regard to normal scale patterns (i.e., the "wild type" of scalation on koi), the N gene is dominant. A non-scale pattern, which is recessive, is designated n. Just looking at a koi with scales will not tell you anything about its genetic makeup for scalation. In other words, a koi can have normal scalation, but its genotype could be one of two types: NN or Nn. The NN koi is termed a *purebred*, as it always will pass on the dominant

trait for normal scales. However, the Nn type, which is *hybrid* (not purebred), can sometimes pass on the gene for normal scalation and sometimes pass on the gene that expresses itself as a lack of scales. A koi that is scaleless must have a genotype of nn.

Assume that you breed two koi with the normal scale pattern. The male is purebred for scalation (NN) while the female, which also presents a normal scalation phenotype, has the hybrid genotype (Nn). What type of offspring could be expected from such a mating?

The mating of these two types of koi would result in a theoretical probability of 50 percent of the spawn being purebred for the dominant scale pattern (NN) and 50% (Nn) hybrid for the scale pattern. No scaleless fishes would be found in the offspring. They would all appear as normal scaled koi. However, some would be carrying the "scaleless" (n) gene.

Now assume that a male of the non-purebred (Nn) genotype is bred with the same female. The offspring would be quite different. The theoretical result would be 25 percent purebred scaled koi (NN), 50 percent nonpurebred scaled koi (Nn), and 25 percent pure scaleless koi (nn).

The above examples should give you an idea of how traits are passed on to koi offspring. Of course, this example is quite basic, but it serves our purpose as an introductory discussion. It becomes more complicated when more than one trait is inherited. Imagine many types of traits being inherited simultaneously and the number of possible phenotypic combinations of the offspring become immense.

Purchasing and Transporting Koi

Selecting your first koi will be exciting and fun. However, care must be exercised in planning for the transport of koi to get them home safely. You will want to make sure that your quarantine facility, whether a container such as a tank or a small pond, is functioning and ready to go before you actually go get them. The following information will ensure that you select healthy koi and transport them properly.

Purchasing Koi

The various sources of koi include pet shops, garden centers, koi farms, individual breeders, and other koi enthusiasts. Whenever possible you will want to personally select the koi yourself.

There are a number of facilities that specialize in breeding koi. Some of these are strictly wholesale businesses that will not sell directly to the public, but a larger operation will be more likely to have a wide range of varieties and price ranges. By all means talk with the breeder before you buy. There will be no better source of information on the fish. Use this book to prepare a list of questions to ask, and make sure you get good answers. You will want to know all about their genealogy, characteristics, value and quality, disease resistance, feeding habits, etc. Make sure you get all the details on fish and pond maintenance. Write it all down. Don't be afraid to stand there and take notes. The breeder has the information you need.

If you do not have a breeder nearby, or if you find yourself taken with the products of some distant operation, make sure you've spent enough time on the telephone talking with the breeder. In addition to all the history and maintenance questions mentioned above, ask about their shipping arrangements. Air freight is the normal shipping mode for all but very short hauls. You will need to get a firm arrival date, because you will want to be on hand when your fish arrive.

Koi can also be purchased from pet stores and pond and garden centers, but the selection at these establishments may be highly variable. Their advantage is convenience: There are a multitude of outlets all over the country. Once again, make sure you ask the relevant questions and get the answers you need to make an intelligent selection.

Tip: There are individual koi enthusiasts who routinely breed their fish. They will usually have too many fish on their hands at hatching time. The best way to locate these individuals is to find out about local koi clubs or associations. Such clubs sponsor area lectures and koi sales, and participate in competitions and other events at national and international levels. The associations offer a wealth of information on koi care and about where to purchase koi and other pond related items.

Evaluating Koi

You should examine each fish, making sure it is free of damage. Look for lesions, fungus, nodules, or swellings.

The fish should have a normal breathing pattern and should not be scratching on the bottom of the tank.

Ask about the following:

• The quality of the water in which the fish are being held, including pH, hardness and temperature.

• What types of food the fish are being fed, frequency of feeding, and quantity fed.

• The age of the fish and whether they were bred at the farm or were imported.

• Whether the fish have been quarantined and treated for possible disease. This is especially important if the fish have recently been imported, as most such fish are carrying some type of disease agent. Flukes and protozoans are very common on imported koi.

• If the koi were treated for disease, ask if the disease was identified prior to treatment, the type of chemicals used, and the dosage and duration of the treatment.

No matter what has happened before you acquired the fish, it is recommended that you still quarantine the fish after transporting them back to your pond as a precautionary measure.

Packing and Shipping

Your fish should be placed in appropriate heavy-duty plastic bags with an ample quantity of aerated water. The bags should then be placed in a styrofoam container to maintain their temperature during transport. Packed properly, the koi can safely remain in this bag for at least 24 hours after purchase from a local supplier. However, the shorter the time the fish remain in the bag the better. Keep in mind that ammonia and carbon dioxide begin to build up in the bag as the fish respire.

In addition, the longer the fish are in the bag, the greater the increase in the bacterial load. If the fish are carrying disease agents such as protozoans, such water conditions will favor their multiplication, and they will be able to attack the fish more easily.

If your koi are only going to be in the transport bag for a few hours, it is unnecessary to add any medications. However, you should add some common (noniodized) salt to produce a concentration of about 0.05 percent, 4 teaspoons per gallon (20 grams per 3.78 L). This concentration is low enough that it will not harm the fish, but will reduce stress associated with handling. An alternative is to use a multipurpose water conditioner such as Kordon's Novaqua.

If the koi are to remain in the bag for a longer period or overnight, it is suggested that additional steps be taken. First, add a commercial ammonia detoxifier. These products are able to bind any toxic forms of ammonia into a nontoxic form. They will significantly reduce the possibility of problems when used in shipping bags. Secondly, consider adding a medication to reduce the possibility of infection during the transport period. Ask the breeder for advice. It is not recommended that antibiotics be added to the water during the transport period. Rather, use parasiticides that also exert an antibacterial effect, such as acriflavine, malachite green, or formalin/malachite combinations.

Finally, never overcrowd shipping bags. Do not mix substantially different sizes of fish in the same bag. Larger fish should be placed individually in bags, while several smaller juveniles can be placed together.

Short-haul Transport

The moving of fish from a shipping bag to a quarantine tank is only one procedure that you will be using. Once your pond is in operation, you will need to move fish on occasion from pond to holding tank and back for various reasons, such as treatment of sick fish or for cleaning the entire pond.

Moving koi from a large pond can be quite difficult. It will involve the use of additional equipment to capture and restrain the fish. While nets can be safely used to move smaller koi, they can cause extensive damage to the skin and can initiate bacterial infections. Therefore, avoid their use whenever possible.

Nets are, nevertheless, essential tools of koi husbandry. They should be carefully selected to minimize problems during capture and transport.

Choose only shallow, fine- to medium-mesh nets. The large, wide mesh nets sold in sporting goods stores are unsuitable. The fish's fins will get caught and damaged.

The following procedure illustrates the moving of koi from one pond to another or to a quarantine facility.

First, carefully lower the pond water slightly to allow for better observation and to make it easier to spot the particular fish you wish to move. If you have potted plants in the pond you may wish to carefully remove them.

Get your barrier net ready. At least two people will be required to manipulate it. Stretch the barrier net across one

Packing koi for transport should be done carefully. After removal from the pond or container, add well-aerated water and secure the top of the bag. Place the koi in a covered styrofoam box to prevent rapid temperature changes.

end of the pond. Slowly draw the net across the pond, herding the fish ahead of you. Do not confine them too closely.

Next, take a large plastic pail or large, clean garbage bucket, submerge it in the pond, and turn it on its side. Buckets with handles are the best choice, especially for moving larger koi.

To release the fish, submerge the bucket and slowly turn it on its side, allowing your charge to swim out naturally. A cover is immediately placed over the enclosure to prevent the fish from jumping out.

Although this method of capturing and transporting koi is more tedious and time-consuming than netting, it minimizes stress to the fish and avoids physical injury.

Repeat the procedure as often as required to move additional koi.

Tip: Never use buckets that have been used for other purposes or that have been washed out with detergents. Purchase new containers that will be used exclusively for your pond.

Using your hand, or a shallow-type net, guide the selected koi into the container. Pour out any excess water, leaving just enough to cover the koi at least an inch or two. Turn the bucket upright and take the fish where you want to go.

Useful Literature and Addresses

Books

Stadelmann, Peter *Water Gardens, Barron's Educational Series, Inc.,* Hauppauge, New York: 1992.

Riemer, D.N. *Guide to Freshwater Vegetation.* AVI Publishing, Westport, Connecticut: 1982.

Waite, T.D. *Principles of Water Quality.* Academic Press, New York, New York: 1984.

Publications

Koi USA. Published bimonthly by the Associated Koi Clubs of America, Midway City, California, 92655.

Pondscapes. Published monthly by The Pond Society, Acworth, Georgia 30101.

Freshwater and Marine Aquarium Magazine. Published monthly by RC Modeler, Sierra Madre, California 91024.

Fish, Plants and Supplies

Your local pet store and garden center should be able to satisfy most of your needs for fish, plants, and supplies. However, if you experience difficulty with particular requirements, you might wish to contact any of the following mail order houses.

Van Ness Water Gardens
  2460 North Euclid Avenue
  Upland, California 91786.

Lilypons Water Gardens
  6800 Lilypons Road
  Lilypons, Maryland 21717.

Blue Ridge Fish Hatchery
(specialists in butterfly koi)
  4536 Kernersville Road
  Kernersville, North Carolina
  27284.

Golden State Fisheries
  10190 Florin Road
  Sacramento, California 95829

Index